PREPARE THE WAY

ROBERT STEARNS

PREPARE THE WAY by Robert Stearns
Published by Creation House
Strang Communications Company
600 Rinehart Road
Lake Mary, Florida 32746
www.creationhouse.com
www.charismalife.com

Unless otherwise noted, all Scripture quotations are from the Holy Bible, New International Version. Copyright © 1973, 1978, 1984, International Bible Society. Used by permission.

Scripture quotations marked KJV are from the King James Version of the Bible.

Scripture quotations marked NKJV are from the New King James Version of the Bible. Copyright © 1979, 1980, 1982, by Thomas Nelson, Inc., publishers. Used by permission.

Library of Congress Cataloging-in-Publication Data:
Stearns, Robert.
  Prepare the way / Robert Stearns
    p. cm.
  ISBN: 0-88419-630-5
  1. Spiritual life—Christianity. 2. Religious awakening— Christianity. 3. Church renewal. I. Title.
BV4501.2.S7574   1999
243—dc21   99-26043
                                                      CIP

9 0 1 2 3 4 5 BBG 8 7 6 5 4 3 2 1
Printed in the United States of America

For Loretta, who prays...

Acknowledgments

Writing a book, I have found, is not an easy task. There are many who have helped this vision come to pass. I will not be able to thank them all, but I would like to acknowledge some of them.

My grandmother, Ronnie Rosar, continues to bless my life as a wonderful example of Christ's unconditional love.

I would like to thank the wonderful team at Eagles' Wings for their vision and support, and especially thank David Trementozzi, Michael Fickess and Derek Johnson, who assisted directly in the process.

While I was writing, Buck and Elaine Petty provided wonderful hospitality in their mountain home in Moravian Falls, North Carolina.

My life and our ministry have been blessed with a tremendous Advisory Board, and I would like to thank Larry Kreider, Don Finto, Dan Juster, Steve Fry, Michael Sullivant and David Rudolph for their wisdom, example and dedication.

I am grateful to Steve Strang and Creation House for their patience with, and belief in, this first-time author.

Finally, I want to deeply thank all the members of the Impact Destiny Team who have stood as supporters with Eagles' Wings for the past several years as our vision has unfolded. Without your prayers and financial support, this would not have come to pass.

May the Lord bless you all a hundredfold for your faithfulness.

Contents

~

Foreword

~

Every so often there comes along a book, song or message that captures part of God's heart for the moment and gives voice to the thoughts and purposes being stirred in a generation. I believe *Prepare the Way* by Robert Stearns is such a book and such a message.

Emerging across the body of Christ today is a John the Baptist cry, preparing a way for the Messiah. I call it the forerunner spirit. Those friends of the Bridegroom who realize the immanence of His return are being motivated as never before by an inner compulsion to prepare their hearts and God's house for the Lord's soon return.

Robert Stearns is one such voice who is mobilizing parts of the body for the purposes of the Lord in this hour. Through his music, his teaching, Eagles' Wings conferences and now through this timely book, Robert is a catalyst for stirring the body and releasing the power of the Holy Spirit in this generation.

By identifying strategic themes that transcend denominational or cultural barriers, Robert Stearns brings forth a message from the heart of the Lord in this book that will awaken in hearts a passion for the Lord and the things on His heart. Some also will be called to serve as watchmen to the part of the body of Christ to which they relate, calling them to be "sons of Issachar," with the ability to properly discern the times and seasons in which we have been privileged to live.

I encourage those with a heart to be current with the word of the Lord to this generation to read this book and let it be a tool of the Lord in your life. Allow it to become an inspiration to wholehearted discipleship.

—MIKE BICKLE
FRIENDS OF THE BRIDEGROOM
KANSAS CITY, MO

Introduction

~

This is a book about change. It is about change that is occurring, and must occur, for the church of Jesus Christ to move into our destiny. Radical change is occurring all around us, in every facet of life—economic, environmental, political, cultural and technological. If you are not aware of it, then you are ignoring it. Faster-paced and more dramatic change is going to come. It will impact our lives—your life—in substantial life-altering ways. You can ignore this fact and deal with the change when it comes as best you can. Or you can prepare now for what will happen.

The church will change because it must if we will survive. And we will survive, because Jesus has promised that the "gates of hell shall not prevail against it" (Matt. 16:18, KJV). But we must understand that it is the *true church* that will survive and, I believe, move into its finest hour. The true church—not all the institutions, traditions, mind-sets and trappings we currently call and understand as church.

Church life is being and will be radically redefined. Radical change to church life—your church life—is coming. You can ignore this fact and deal with the change when it comes as best you can. Or you can begin now to participate in what is, without question, the most exciting and unparalleled time in church history since the Book of Acts.

There is no middle ground, no compromise, no spectators and no bystanders. It is simply a matter of time before events force believers and local fellowships into situations that will reveal our depth, our substance and our authenticity. We can choose now to turn our face into the winds of change and let the blowing and shaking begin. If we do, we will have the joy of intentionally participating early on with the greatest reformation and resulting harvest in the history of the church. If not, we will be bewildered, feel betrayed by God and our leaders and wonder why no one told us to get ready for what was coming. You are being told now. Get ready. Change is coming. In fact, from this point on, the only constancy...is change.

AN OVERVIEW

Having traveled constantly around the world over the past several years, I have been privileged to relate to a wide variety of the body of Christ. Though I come from a Pentecostal/charismatic context, I have been blessed to meet and work with wonderful brothers and sisters from all backgrounds of the body of Christ. As the years have passed, I have begun to notice a pattern. I have seen that many times the same themes are being presented and discussed in diverse parts of the body, even those parts that do not "cross-pollinate" naturally. These themes, properly understood, become signposts, helping us along the way. Many times, these themes are presented in different terms or ecclesiastical languages, but when you get to the essence of them, they are the same. It is as if the Holy Spirit is speaking the same message to the church simultaneously, but incarnating the message within particular church cultures.

I began to feel compelled by the Lord to offer this book as a broad perspective, in language that is as inclusive as possible, targeting twelve key themes that I believe the Holy Spirit is emphasizing to the body as a whole right now. These are certainly not the only things God is saying, but I have seen that in whatever place in the body I find myself, many or most of these themes are being emphasized. The goal in pinpointing these spiritual signposts, or trends, is that we would not only become aware that they are happening, but would begin to ardently seek the Lord as to how we are to respond to what He is saying.

HOW TO READ THIS BOOK

The goal of this book is that it will at the same time speak loudly to the corporate body and intensely to the individual believer. Here are some practical insights as to the nature and flow of the book that will help you get the most from reading it.

INFORMATION AND INSPIRATION

Different people are motivated by different things. Some are motivated by information, which speaks to the mind and gives a compelling, cognitive reason to move ahead. Others are moved by their heart and need to feel something strongly before it changes their course of action.

In this book, I have endeavored to offer both information and inspiration. I wanted to be careful that none of the themes I presented were simply personal "soap box" issues, so I searched through the body to be sure that there were many different leaders from a variety of backgrounds currently speaking to these same issues. For those readers drawn to information, there is a basic level of evidence offered to support the claims being made and a healthy Notes section to direct you to further resources. For those who respond to the heart, I endeavored consistently to yield myself to the Lord and allow His voice to flow through me. I trust that as you read, the Lord will confirm many things you have been sensing in your heart but perhaps not yet been able to put words to.

INDIVIDUAL AND CORPORATE

Throughout the book you will find questions at the end of each chapter. There are group and individual tasks, some interchangeable. There will be some questions and tasks that can be accomplished in an hour or so, but many will require prayer, the grace of the Lord and time for newly planted seeds to grow. Do not try to take on too much at once, but instead focus on a chapter at a time, coming back to tasks when you are prepared.

One goal is that this book would give clarity and acceleration to these unfolding purposes of the Lord. These questions make this book especially useful as a tool for your Sunday school class or home group. It will challenge your paradigms and hopefully motivate you to personal and corporate change.

> Blessed is the man whose strength is in You, whose heart is set on pilgrimage. As they pass through the Valley of Baca, they make it a spring; the rain also covers it with pools. They go from strength to strength; each one appears before God in Zion.
>
> —PSALM 84:5–7, NKJV

Coming to personal faith in Christ, or "getting saved," does not mean our journey is over. It means it has just begun. We are the company of those who seek the city whose builder and maker is God. We are marching through time to an eternal home. It is Zion, the city of God, where the law of His supreme, holy love rules the land.

Where are you on your journey? There is a highway we are traveling on called the Highway of Holiness. My prayer is that this book will help prepare the way for the Lord in our hearts, our homes, our cities and nations. May it be a spiritual compass to help you accurately find your location and point you in your future direction!

—ROBERT STEARNS
APRIL 21, 1999
YOM HAATZMUT
ISRAEL INDEPENDENCE DAY
JERUSALEM, ISRAEL

1

Passion for Jesus

*The next generation will have an
earnest, abandoned passion for Jesus and little or
no tolerance for lifeless religion.*

After ministering at a Sunday morning service at a church in Florida, I was preparing to go out to a restaurant with the pastor and his family. The pastor suggested his fifteen-year-old son ride in my car so that if we became separated in traffic his son could direct me to the restaurant.

We got in the car. I glanced over at the teenager—baggy jeans and a t-shirt, three or four earrings and hair that was a unique shade of green. We started the drive in silence. I wondered if he would be interested in conversation. I began wondering how long it would take to get to the restaurant.

Breaking the silence, I said, "So, do you have any hobbies? What do you like to do? What makes you tick?"

His answer came, clear, vulnerable and powerful in its simplicity. "Loving Jesus," he said.

In a moment, my perspective changed.

Paramount to every other trend in this book is the fact that everywhere the church is rediscovering Jesus. Traditional, lifeless, religious motions are being replaced by a vibrant sense of the availability of a living, dynamic relationship with this glorious person, Jesus, the Messiah.

RELIGION VS. SPIRITUALITY

We are living in the midst of a spiritual awakening.

Unfortunately, it is happening largely outside the church of Jesus Christ.

Someone has said, "Religion is someone who has not had an experience with God telling other people who have not had an experience with God about people who had an experience with God."

There has perhaps never been a more sinister plot concocted in the depths of hell to keep men from God than the spirit of religion. Of course, this is not true religion, which James defines for us as visiting the fatherless and the widow and keeping ourselves pure from the spirit of this world, but the vain, hypocritical religious spirit that Jesus attacked in the Pharisees. (See James 1:27; Matthew 23.)

If religion could attract the unchurched masses and really impact those who faithfully attend church, then America would certainly be in much better shape. Unfortunately, the statistics show that the world perceives the institutional church as irrelevant. The nominal Christian cycles around from church to church throughout his city or town without ever being established in a true discipling context where life issues can be addressed and Christian growth can take place. George Barna notes:

> Average attendance in mainline Protestant churches has dropped to just ninety-eight adults.[1]

In the midst of this, however, we see spiritism and the New Age movement at an all-time high. The most successful movies and television programs include angels or the supernatural. Psychic telephone hot lines proliferate. Western society at the end of the twentieth century is groping beyond the shallow materialism of the past fifty years and yearning again for a deep spiritual foundation. The hedonism of the sixties and seventies and materialism of the eighties have produced a generation that knows there must be more because they have seen a basic meaninglessness to their parents' lives. They are wanting and willing to "sell out" for anything that answers the need of their hearts.

Unfortunately, most of this generation grew up in some kind of Sunday school setting in a church that they drifted from in their late teen or college years. They have no thought that the church can provide any real answers. Many cannot get over the hypocrisy they have seen in their parents' lives. Others have been disillusioned by moral failures from spiritual leaders. They believe they have tried Christianity, and it has failed to answer their needs for a spiritual reality, and so they go looking elsewhere. George Barna comments:

> The Busters Generation [born between 1965 and 1983] have shown an inclination to reject church right from the start. The result: slowly declining church attendance among the adult population. Millions of them have rejected churches because of the perceived lack of relevance and sensitivity of churches to human need.[2]

I had an experience recently that brought this trend home to me, literally. As a child, I used to attend Vacation Bible School every summer in a little, idyllic American village church near my home. Our town was far from any big city, with very little pluralism or multi-ethnicity. I remember going to these summer Bible lessons, playing with friends and learning basic Bible stories.

Recently I happened to be driving in that same quaint, old neighborhood and thought I would drive by this small country church that was such a source of memories of my early spiritual formation.

As I approached the church, I noticed that the cross was no longer on the top of the steeple. I slowed my car at the front of the building and read the sign. It said "Center for the Practice of Eastern Religion." Whatever happened to small-town Judeo-Christian heritage? America is changing!

AND DELIVER US FROM ... RELIGION

Religion is insidious because it reduces the supreme loving, liberating force in the universe to a series of "oughts and "shoulds" that have no power to produce true change in a life. It sounds like a cliché, but it is true that the greatest power in the world is love. The source of pure love is God. But religion has portrayed God as a harsh, unloving taskmaster who is more concerned with actions than attitudes. God certainly does care about actions, but Scripture is crystal clear that a holy life flows out of a pure and clean heart. Jesus taught us that the sick need a doctor, not the well (Luke 5:31). King David wrote, "Behold, You desire truth in the inward parts, and in the hidden part You will make me to know wisdom" (Ps. 51:6, NKJV).

Dead religion, this plot of hell, has deep and long-lasting impact. For example, one of the most difficult areas in the world today for evangelism is post-Reformation Europe. Europe, once the home to holy revolutionaries like Wycliffe, Hus, Luther, Knox, Wesley and others, has been so burned out on religion that Christianity is essentially regarded with cold indifference, and paganism is on the rise.

I believe the next generation will not tolerate a Christianity that is not wholly authentic. There will simply not be time or effort invested in churches or institutions that sound and look shallow and plastic. There is a tremendous anointing of *discernment* on this generation, even those not consciously in relationship with God. They possess an instinctive quest for the real thing. This discernment ferrets out insincerity and thirsts for the genuine.

This generation will have the blessing of honesty. They will *not* prophesy "peace, peace...when there is no peace" just to maintain a status quo Sunday morning service. (See Jeremiah 6:14.) They would rather admit spiritual emptiness and desperation and begin before God *and one another* in a place of honesty than play the part of the counselors' lauding the emperor's new clothes. A hunger for a real individual and corporate spiritual life will become their driving force. It will replace the deeply inbred "ought" of going through religious motion. It will release a cry and demand lifted up in the land for life.

Heaven answers those kind of prayers.

This will have tremendous impact on the institutional church. This driving thirst for spiritual life will directly oppose the apathetic deadwood who want to maintain church as usual. Pastors and boards will be presented with a terrible quandry. The present church leadership, seeking survival, may decide simply to placate the faithfully attending and tithing Sunday morning crowd. But they will soon realize that the church will have no future because neither guilt nor tradition will bring the next generation to church on Sunday morning. The next generation will simply stop attending, and the church will be left with a docile, obedient, but shrinking older crowd with no generation to pass anything on to.

The following quotation is from Wade Clark Roof:

> Greater numbers of young Americans adhere to what is described as the 'new volunteerism': church is a matter of choice, less a socially ascribed or cultural expectation.[3]

In the midst of this crisis, the next generation will discover *Jesus.*

INTIMACY WITH JESUS

The church is coming to a place where relationship with Jesus is really all that matters.

Many aspects of Christ's message vie for our attention. There is so much in the Word to learn! But too often we have succumbed to focusing our attention on one aspect of Jesus' teaching rather than developing a relationship with the Teacher. This misplaced focus leads us to all kinds of church movements that divide and weaken us. So we have portions of the church that focus on healing, some on faith, some on evangelism or spiritual warfare. The list is endless. All these, and many other areas of focus, are valid and necessary aspects of the Christian life. But all too often these teachings become the filter by which we define our Christian lives. Instead, we must constantly keep the plumb line of simple devotion to Jesus. If we get stuck on a pet teaching or doctrine, we are on the road to inward fruitlessness and outward powerlessness.

We must regularly experience the penetrating gaze of Jesus' eyes. Through the power of His Spirit, He searches our hearts, jealous over our affection. If we do not have these times of truly experiencing Him, then anything—our ministry, our theology, all our good activities—can easily become an idol, keeping us from deep relationship with the very One we say we are serving.

Mike Bickle, the leader of Metro Christian Fellowship in Kansas City, Missouri, is a primary voice calling the church back to the place of first love. He wrote:

> The enemy has assaulted the people of God. He has weakened and destroyed our foundation of the knowledge of God. He has sought to defeat us by diluting our passion for Jesus and diverting us from our divine purpose. Satan has done his job well. But in His arsenal God has reserved the secret weapon of all the ages—the awesome knowledge of the splendor of the person of Jesus. The blazing light and majestic loveliness of the knowledge of God are about to shine into the community of the redeemed, and all the dark forces of hell will not be able to overpower it.
>
> The splendor and glory of Jesus Christ will capture the affections of the church in a new way. Compromise and passivity will be solved as the Lord allows us to gaze upon Him with deeper insight into His personal beauty and glory. The body of Christ will rediscover Christ's personhood and majesty. When we do, we will give ourselves to Him in unparalled affection and obedience.[4]

THE HEART OF MARY—CHOOSING PURE DEVOTION

We all know the story. Jesus has come to town to visit with His friends Lazarus, Martha and Mary. The arrival of Jesus and His entourage have set Martha and her performance-oriented soul into a flurry of activity. There is so much to do! She has such a desire that things be just right for the Rabbi.

In the midst of this bustle, she can't find her sister anywhere. When she finally realizes her sister is sitting at Jesus' feet and not helping at all, anger boils inside her. At first she brushes it aside, determining not to let it show. She will confront Mary later. But quickly the tension grows as she feels the frustration of Mary's insensitivity to her needs. She blurts out her anger to the Lord, and He utters those famous words that strike deeply in my soul every time I consider them.

> Martha, Martha...you are worried and upset about many things, but only one thing is needed. Mary has chosen what is better, and it will not be taken away from her.
>
> —LUKE 10:41–42

I believe the Holy Spirit is releasing to the church in this hour the heart of Mary—a simple belief that pure devotion to Him will bring true, lasting, personal change, which will then result in societal impact. This is our beginning place. This is the source of our activity. This is the place to which we seek to draw men and women—not to a system or institution or program—but to a real place at the feet of Jesus, near to His heart.

It has been wonderful to see this movement back to first love, which is evidenced in popular worship songs.

> My Jesus, my Savior, Lord, there is none like you.
> All of my days, I want to praise the wonders of Your mighty love.
> My comfort, my shelter, tower of refuge and strength,
> Let every breath, all that I am, never cease to worship You![5]

> Jesus, Jesus,
> Holy and anointed one, Jesus.[6]

> Lord, I give You my heart; I give You my soul.
> I live for You alone.
> Every breath that I take, every moment I'm awake,
> Lord, have Your way in me.[7]

Jesus, lover of my soul,
Jesus, I will never let You go.
You've taken me from the miry clay,
You've set my feet upon the Rock, and now I know
I love You; I need You.
Though my world may fall I'll never let You go.
My Savior, my closest friend,
I will worship You until the very end.[8]

So many of the songs congregations around the world are singing right now are not just songs about the Lord, but powerful love songs directly to the Lord. By the sheer vulnerability of their words, these songs invite the worshiper into a place of intimacy with Christ.

This is causing us to ask, Who really is Jesus?

MR. SPOCK VS. THE DALI LAMA

Jesus was the most radical man of His day. He was not a politician or diplomat. His most stinging rebukes never came to sinners. They always came to the religious.

Jesus will emerge as a hero to this generation. They will see Him as their champion. As the power of the Holy Spirit draws true believers deeper into a discovery of the person of Christ in all of His power, His compassion, His humanity, His mysticism, they will begin to see, know, and present Jesus as He truly is.

He is, quite simply, the most radical figure on the stage of human history. Keanu Reeves recently starred in a movie as the young Buddha. Why is Hollywood so intrigued with Eastern mystic characters? Why does one of Hollywood's biggest stars do a movie about Buddha, while the only recent treatment Hollywood has given to Jesus is the blasphemy of *The Last Temptation of Christ?*

Partly, at least, it is because the Western church has presented a Western, religious, demystified Jesus.

JESUS, THE RELEVANT MYSTIC

The Western world, framed in Aristotelian rationalism, has enthroned logic and shunned experience, either physical or spiritual, as a basis for truth. It is becoming increasingly obvious, even to secular psychologists and sociologists, that sheer rationalism is simply insufficient to be the sole grid for measuring human experience. This is evidenced by the incredible increase of the New Age movement.

> In turbulent times...of great change, people head for...personal spiritual experience. With no membership lists or even a coherent philosophy or dogma, it is difficult to define or measure the unorganized New Age movement. But in every major U.S. and European city thousands who seek insight and personal growth cluster around a metaphysical bookstore or spiritual teacher.[9]

Why don't our churches show Jesus as the mystic that the Scriptures and history show Him to be? Many times Jesus spoke of Himself as a seer, a prophet. He spoke of an inner, mystical communion with God out of which all of His life activity flowed.

> I tell you the truth, the Son can do nothing by himself; he can do only what he sees his Father doing, because whatever the Father does the Son also does.
>
> —JOHN 5:19

Simply taking those words at face value shows us that Christ had a deep sense of living out of mystical vision and experiential communion with God, His Father. We may not like that description, and those words may sound New Age to us. But if we follow the simplest hermeneutics (Bible interpretation), we see that Jesus was a mystic and lived that way.

His mysticism, however, did not divorce Him from the real world. Rather, it made Him more relevant to it than ever, as any pure mystical discipline should. He was not "so heavenly minded that He was no earthly good." In fact, His choice of location for His first miracle was not a synagogue or the Temple, but a wedding. And His first recorded miracle was not centered on a deeply moral or spiritual situation. No, the King of the universe decided that forever recorded in Scripture as His first manifestation of supernatural ability would be getting some wine for a wedding and helping the host save face. What an incredible thing! (See John 2:1–11.)

Who could accuse Mother Theresa of not being relevant, of not being a part of the real world? This deeply spiritual and mystical woman communed with Christ in the rank filth of the poorest of the poor. She shines as a modern-day example of simple devotion to Jesus resulting in profound social and evangelistic work leading to societal transformation.

We in the church must marry mysticism and relevance in our minds. Confronting demons, healing the sick, talking to God, playing with children, attending parties—these were all part of the life of the biblical Jesus. These activities should fit on one list without difficulty because the God we serve is all encompassing. He is the God of all of it—every aspect of our lives.

GOD WITH US

Simply put, the church must become "spiritual" and stop being "religious." However, I want to be clear that the church shouldn't make this change solely because society is shifting that way and we are reacting to our culture. The church should become spiritual rather than religious because our Leader is a mystical, visionary prophet, whose mysticism led Him to embrace little children and overturn religious money handlers; to forgive whores and infuriate priests; to attend parties with sinners and cause a ruckus in church. This is our Emmanual. This generation will refuse to accept a false and limiting projection of Christ any more. (See Luke 18:15–17; Mark 11:15–18; John 8:2–11; Matthew 11:16–19.)

NEITHER DO I CONDEMN THEE

Jesus so infuriated the religious leaders that they put Him to death because He threatened the spirit of control they were exercising over the people. *Religious people always control through fear. Spiritual people always liberate through love.* From Zaccheus to Nicodemus to Mary Magdalene, wherever Jesus saw sincerity, He honored it.

Many of us today would say, "I would do the same thing! If a sinner came to me seeking truth and forgiveness, I would pray with them and love them into the kingdom." The problem is, they are not coming to us. Why is that? Why don't they come to us, and why did they come to Jesus?

First of all, many times He went *to them.* He was not dwelling solely in the temple. The Bible records that Jesus attended weddings and parties and had dinner with tax collectors. He had conversations with women of ill repute, which was certainly unacceptable behavior for a Jewish rabbi. We see Him in the marketplace and enjoying the countryside. We rarely see Him in the temple. We see Him, rather, spending lots of time in ordinary places with ordinary people.

This generation will not wait for the world to come to the building we have erroneously called *the church.* We spend countless hours and huge amounts of money presenting evangelistic programs in our churches that can never compete with the entertainment the world can provide. We must remember that the world is starving for community and relationship—not a better show. What would happen if the next time our church wanted to sponsor an evangelistic campaign to get people saved we did it by inviting our neighbors over for dinner?

But however Jesus encountered these unbelievers, the key to their hearts was that Jesus was *accessible* to them and did not *condemn* them. Do you remember His response to the adulteress about to be stoned? "Woman, where are those accusers of yours?...Neither do I condemn you; go and sin no more" (John 8:10–11, NKJV).

Does our church culture allow sinners to feel that Jesus is accessible and uncondemning to the seeker who is sincere, but not yet a believer? While I am all for civil responsibility and involvement, I fear that some Christians involved in the political process are sounding more like the Pharisees. We loudly proclaim our righteousness and the world's damnation, but we are called to show forth the mercy and grace of a God whose love washes the filth from our own souls on a daily basis. We must remember that we have received the ministry of reconciliation. (See 2 Corinthians 5:18–19.)

What was it about Jesus that made a sinner feel safe enough to let down his defenses, to admit freely his need for cleansing? The sinner knows he is a sinner and needs cleansing. His own God-given image and soul testify against him in the recesses of his heart. What the sinner is looking for is a Savior whose love is powerful enough to deliver and safe enough to trust. That is what people found in Jesus.

IN HIS PRESENCE

In Your presence is fullness of joy; at Your right hand are pleasures forevermore.

—PSALM 16:11, NKJV

We quote this verse, but what does it mean? Where, or what, is the presence of the Lord? How do we experience the living presence of Jesus?

Seven out of ten Christians (70%) say they have never experienced God's presence at a church service.[10]

What a staggering statistic! What is it that we have to offer the world if we don't have the presence of the Lord?

Let us rediscover the presence of Jesus! He is real, and He is waiting for us—His people—to come to the simplicity of celebrating Him! Whatever our denomination, whatever our doctrine, let us seek the place of devotion to Him. Let all of our service, all of our activity, all of our life be subordinated to this one desire... a desire for His presence. Hear these voices from Scripture calling for His presence.

If your Presence does not go with us, do not send us up from here. How will anyone know that you are pleased with me and your people unless you go with us? What else will distinguish me and your people from all the other people on the face of the earth?

—Exodus 13:15–16

One thing have I desired of the Lord, that will I seek after; that I may dwell in the house of the Lord all the days of my life, to behold the beauty of the the Lord, and to inquire in his temple.

—Psalm 27:4, kjv

That I may know Him and the power of his resurrection, and the fellowship of His sufferings.

—Philippians 3:10, nkjv

Moses, David and Paul—three voices raised in holy desperation in pursuit of the presence of the living God. All three were men of action, men of activity, men who led nations and changed history. Yet at the core of their being, there was a cry for His holy presence.

Around the world today the same cry is being raised in the hearts and spirits of believers who are abandoned in passionate pursuit of God. His love has fully captured their hearts. A generation with the heart of Mary is being intoxicated with a love so wonderful, so real, that it melts our defenses and causes us to desire more and more to sit at His feet.

From that place at His feet, our teaching has new clarity; our evangelism has new fervor. Our small groups have deeper vulnerability; our worship reaches higher heights. Our warfare has greater authority; our ministry stems from deeper compassion. Our prayer has greater sincerity; our lives prove greater authenticity.

Like the teenager at the beginning of the chapter, our pursuits and activities are being streamlined to one glorious purpose—*loving Jesus.*

What Now?

For group discussion:

1. Someone has said that the main thing is to keep the main thing the main thing. How can we as the church be sure that our primary focus is growing in living relationship with the Lord?

2. Discuss the difference between religion and spirituality. What scriptural models can we look at to discern between the two? How did Jesus react to the dead religious system?

3. Individually look up a portion of scripture that reveals something of the personality or character of God. Read the scripture aloud to the group.

For personal application:

1. When was the last time outside of a church service you spoke simply with God from your heart?

2. In what ways do you battle with a tendency toward rules and regulations over relationship in your own life?

3. Sit down in a quiet place and write a letter to Jesus, as simply as you would write one to a friend.

2

Ears to Hear

*God is raising up a generation that is
rediscovering the need and joy of hearing the voice
of the Lord. They will be empowered by the inner voice of
the Spirit and grounded in the Word.*

$\mathbf{D}$o you remember this old commercial? The camera pans from an office, to a busy sidewalk, to a cocktail party. All of a sudden, people grow silent and focus their attention on someone we can't see. Then an authoritative voice calmly explains: "When E. F. Hutton talks, people listen."

It is clear that the world is listening for answers. While society breaks down, there is a hope that "Somebody up there is watching out for us."

Evidence of this is as close as your nightly television shows. Movies, sitcoms and dramas such as *Touched by an Angel* show an openness to supernatural intervention. Psychic hotlines are everywhere. Check out the New Age section at your local bookstore. No longer is it just a few isolated shelves! Shelf after shelf is filled with books by gurus channeling messages of hope and direction for the coming millennium. Oprah Winfrey in no longer just a talk show host; she has become a spiritual leader guiding millions into daily meditation, focus and a search for peace and fulfillment.

The evidence is clear—the world is losing hope that our problems can be solved by man's ingenuity or technology. And while many are not convinced of the reality of the supernatural realm, they are willing to give it a shot. The world is going to hear some message as they strain for a voice of hope and direction. Shouldn't it be the voice of the Lord?

Heaven Is Speaking

The entire biblical record of God's dealings with man has one central theme: the message that God loves us and desires relationship with us. He shows that desire by communicating with us as individuals and a collective whole.

Consider these examples:

When Adam and Eve first hid after their sin, the Lord came walking in the cool of the day, calling out softly, "Adam, where are you?" (See Genesis 3:8–9.)

In the wilderness, God found a faithful representative in Moses. The Scripture records, "The Lord would speak to Moses face to face, as a man speaks with his friend" (Exod. 33:11).

King David was at Ziklag in a time of utter despair and defeat. David returned to the heart posture he had maintained since his youth as a shepherd boy. He inquired of the Lord. And, the Scriptures record, the Lord answered him. (See 1 Samuel 30:1–8.)

Jesus, the ultimate Word of God, came to us so that we could see, hear, feel and understand more fully the heart desire of the Father for relationship with His children.

But Jesus' return to heaven did not signal an end to divine communication! He promised us His Spirit who would continue to teach and lead us into all truth.

> But when he, the Spirit of truth, comes, he will guide you into all truth. He will not speak on his own; he will speak only what he hears, and he will tell you what is yet to come.
>
> —John 16:13

I am with you always, to the very end of the age.

—MATTHEW 28:20

Throughout the New Testament, to all kinds of people, through all kinds of means, the voice of the Lord is shown to be speaking. In fact, all of Scripture points toward a belief that God's desire is *not* to speak to only a few select superheroes, but to speak to all His children.

> Come, let us bow down in worship, let us kneel before the LORD our Maker; for he is our God and we are the people of his pasture, the flock under his care. Today, if you hear his voice, do not harden your hearts.
>
> —PSALM 95:6–8

> My sheep listen to my voice; I know them, and they follow me.
>
> —JOHN 10:27

One of the distinctive callings upon this generation is to rediscover and respond to the voice of the Lord. The voice of the Lord is speaking, through all kinds of avenues and in many different ways. Believers everywhere are becoming more sensitive to hear and respond to the voice of the Shepherd.

RELATIONSHIP WITHOUT COMMUNICATION?

Can you imagine any relationship without communication? Essentially, it is impossible. In fact, one of the key ingredients in defining and measuring relationships is communication. How often do you communicate? At what level of vulnerability do you communicate?

Yet, somehow, much of Christianity has bought the lie that God doesn't speak to people today.

Both the Old and New Testament clearly declare that God's voice is being heard and understood even by the nonbeliever, simply through creation.

The heavens declare the glory of God; the skies proclaim the work of his hands. Day after day they pour forth speech; night after night they display knowledge. There is no speech or language where their voice is not heard. Their voice goes out into all the earth, their words to the ends of the world.

—PSALM 19:1–4

Because that which may be known of God is manifest in them [mankind]; for God hath shown it unto them. For the invisible things of him from the creation of the world are clearly seen, being understood by the things that are made, even his eternal power and Godhead; so that they are without excuse: Because that, when they knew God, they glorified him not as God, neither were thankful.

—ROMANS 1:19–21, KJV

Theology clearly teaches us that the world is held accountable because of the natural revelation of God.

Consider this: God sets His voice in the heavens, puts the imprint of His image on man and sets "eternity in their hearts" (Eccles. 3:11, NKJV)—all for the purpose of drawing you into a saving relationship with Himself, your loving heavenly Father...*and then He never speaks to you again until you get to heaven?*

Does that sound ridiculous?

Functionally, this is much of what the church has taught and lived. They believe God spoke to Moses and David and Paul and John the Revelator. And they believe He spoke to your heart enough while you were a sinner to bring you to the point of salvation. But after you are His child, they say you have to be content with reading Bible stories about others who heard His voice. You have to be satisfied with learning good doctrine from these stories because you can't hear the voice of God as they did.

Think of God's pattern of communication with man at a corporate level. God told Abraham He would produce a mighty nation through him; He said through him He would bless all the nations of the earth. (See Genesis 12:1–3.) God revealed Himself to the children of Israel on Mount

Sinai with thunders and lightnings and constant miracles. Then He birthed the church with supernatural experiences in the upper room. The New Testament is full of fabulous accounts of God's supernatural interventions for the church including dreams, visions and prophecies.

Therefore, it makes absolutely no sense to say the last-days church, which will face persecution and unparalled difficulty, will have to be content with what they can cognitively understand through study. Though God's pattern for thousands of years has been regular and dramatic communication with His people, His last-days church will have to make it without His voice.

Isn't that a ludicrous thing to say?

Unfortunately, though few would put it that way, the logical outworking of much of what is taught today in seminaries and pulpits is just that. Sadly, it has left a generation of believers who long for more in their relationship with God but are unable to learn to hear His voice because their conditioning tells them God only speaks today through the study and mental grasping of the written Word.

Let me say this plainly: *God wants to speak to you regularly and help you grow in an understanding of how to hear and respond to His voice. Your prayer times, and your daily living, should be two-way communication.*

Let's consider some testimonies.

SURPRISE!

One significant church leader of our day who had a dramatic paradigm shift in regard to hearing the voice of God is Dr. Jack Deere. Dr. Deere was a professor at Dallas Theological Seminary and well respected in academic circles. His excellent book *Surprised by the Voice of God* does an extremely thorough job of dealing with this important topic that we are briefly touching on in this book. He wrote:

> I was the pastor of a Bible church for a number of years. During that time I did not believe God spoke in any reliable way except through

the Bible…Looking back on that time, I realize now that so much of the Bible actually seemed unreal to me. I had relegated many experiences of the Bible to a distant, unrepeatable past. It had become for me primarily a book of doctrines and abstract truths about God. I loved the doctrines of the Bible and its literary beauty, but I shared very few experiences with the people of the Bible.

Unlike me, the people of the Bible heard God speak in a variety of ways. He spoke through an audible voice, through dreams, visions, circumstances, fleeces, inner impressions, prophets, angels and other ways, as well as through the Scriptures. These things were so common in New Testament times that Paul had to give detailed instructions to the Corinthians concerning the use of prophecy, tongues, words of wisdom, words of knowledge, and even discernment of spirits. (See 1 Corinthians 12–14.) The author of Hebrews even underscored the importance of hospitality, reminding his readers that by showing hospitality "some people have entertained angels without knowing it" (Heb. 13:2). He believed that in his day angelic visits were still possible!

I didn't have to be a theological genius to read the Bible and figure out that God used to speak in many different ways to His people. But after God wrote the Bible, He apparently went mute, or so it seemed to me, for the only way I could hear Him speak was through His book. On a practical level, I acted as though the Holy Spirit was some kind of impersonal force who provided the church with vague, ill-defined, general guidance. Many believers are in this predicament today.[1]

It is wonderful to hear this learned man explain the steps of this glorious discovery of hearing and responding to the voice of God.

In beginning the process of learning [to hear the voice of God] I felt like a little child trying to learn the language of his parents. I did have three things going for me. First, I had an acute sense of my spiritual poverty. I now believed I could not hear the voice of God very well. Second, I had come to believe that God was still speaking in all the ways He spoke in the Bible. And third, I knew I needed God to speak to me in more personal ways if I was ever going to experience the kind of church life described in the New Testament.[2]

ARE YOU JEWISH?

God speaks in many ways, and this generation is learning to hear His voice everywhere, not only in the stillness of our hearts. Consider the testimony of David Trementozzi, my colleague who serves with me at Eagles' Wings.

The first time I met David, he came up and shook my hand after I had ministered at his church in a Sunday morning service. He asked if he could have a few moments to talk with me. Since I had a lunch appointment with friends, I told him that if he didn't mind driving me to where I was having lunch, we could have the time together in the car.

The next words that came out of my mouth were, "Are you Jewish?"

Now, I don't know why I asked that question, except to say that I felt I was responding to an almost subconscious prompting of the Holy Spirit. But when David said he was not Jewish, but Italian, I simply dropped it.

We walked a few steps toward the back of the church, where my friend Ron was waiting. I introduced David (whom I had only known now for about three minutes) to Ron. Ron then looked at David and said, "David, are you Jewish?" David laughed at the seeming coincidence of this question, but I immediately sensed that the Holy Spirit was at work.

David drove me to my lunch appointment, and it became clear during our drive that we needed more time to talk, so he stayed for lunch.We returned for the evening service, where I was to minister. Throughout that evening about five more people asked David if he were Jewish. David questioned me about this, wondering if I were playing some kind of prank on him. I told him that I had not set him up for any prank and that I did not even know some of the people who had asked him this question. I suggested that maybe the Holy Spirit was trying to speak to him. David said that prior to that day, he never recalled anyone ever asking him if he were Jewish.

By this point in our conversation, David had expressed an interest in joining our organization. I recommended that he come up the following weekend to a conference we were hosting in the New York City area; he could then interact with the rest of our staff and get more of a sense of what our ministry does.

Let me say here that a primary thrust of Eagles' Wings is a strong calling and burden for Israel and the Jewish people. From the first few moments I met David, I felt the Lord was calling him to join our team, and so my sense of what was happening was that the Holy Spirit was speaking to David as this same question was being asked over and over. I believed this was both a confirmation to him and me of his coming to Eagles' Wings. It also prepared his heart to receive an understanding and burden for ministry to the Jewish people.

When David arrived in New York City that weekend, he informed me that several more people throughout the week had asked him if he were Jewish. Again, I said nothing, waiting for it to be clear to David that what was happening was supernatural.

The conference that weekend was in a local church that had no specific focus on Israel. As people at the conference would meet David, about ten more asked if he were Jewish. Finally, after one evening service, we went out to eat and there David was introduced to a brother named James for the first time. The first words out of James' mouth were, "Are you Jewish?"

This was it! David, now very frustrated, turned to me and told me that he didn't think this was very funny and that I should stop setting up these incidents. What could I say? I knew what was happening, but much of this prophetic atmosphere was very new to David.

Thankfully, James, a mature brother in the Lord who is familiar with the prophetic realm, stepped in and assured David that he and I had not spoken at all. James and I were then finally able to minister to David that it was clear throughout the week that the Lord was speaking to him and to me through this, preparing David to join our team and grow in his understanding of ministry to Jewish people.

Here was a clear example of the voice of the Lord speaking through a series of divinely inspired circumstances. In this situation, perhaps He was not merely speaking, but shouting! I believe the Lord regularly speaks to us in the midst of circumstances if we will have an ear tuned to hear what He is saying. Sometimes, however, He not only speaks through circumstances, but also through people.

He Knew My Name

One dramatic encounter I had when I first realized the Lord still is speaking today came several years ago through the ministry of a man named Paul Cain. I was attending a conference in Kansas City, Missouri, hosted by Metro Christian Fellowship, where Mike Bickle is the pastor. There were thousands at the conference, and I knew only a handful of people there.

It was only the second time I had heard Paul Cain speak. After his sermon, he began sharing impressions as he received them from the Holy Spirit.

All of a sudden, I heard him say, "And there is a young man here tonight named Robert from Buffalo, New York. You are twenty-three years old, and you lead worship and play the piano." I about fell out of my chair! All of this information was completely accurate. He then began to share words of encouragement from the heart of the Lord to me. This experience came at a crucial time in my life and helped me immensely in persevering toward what the Lord had for me.

The Baby With the Bath Water

Perhaps you are someone who has been around this type of public expression of God's voice and have seen it abused or misused. Perhaps you yourself have been wounded by ministry that has done more harm than good. Clearly there has been a good deal of questionable activity in this area; some have resulted in a tremendous amount of pain and division in the body of Christ. However, having experienced firsthand both the blessings of this ministry and its abuses, I still firmly believe that the Lord is restoring the precious gift of the private and corporate hearing of His voice to His people.

One of the primary reasons these abuses have occurred is that church leaders have not followed biblical procedures for judging these words. This aspect of the church's ministry has stayed immature because it has largely not been pruned and nurtured.

Some humorous examples of this come from years in a Pentecostal Bible college. In the course of four years of daily chapel services, I heard some very well-meaning students get a little confused about what the Lord was saying. I like to call these "prophecies I have heard."

Yea, hath not I, the Lord, said unto you that a bird in the hand is worth two in the bush?

Yea, My children, as I was with Moses in the ark when the waters rose, so shall I be with thee. Oops, I meant Noah.

Yea, My children, I say unto thee yea. Yea, verily, yea...um ...yea...Amen.

O my children, I know you are tired and worn down. You are weary, My children, discouraged and ready to give up. I know because I, the Lord your God, feel the same way Myself sometimes.

These are humorous examples that cause us to chuckle. No doubt these thoughts came from well-meaning people who may even have been receiving a genuine prompting from the Lord to share some word of encouragement with the student body. However, the emotion and pressure of "speaking the word of the Lord" was such that it pushed them to put on a personality that was not their own. They attempted to bolster the authority of what they were saying. We forget that the Holy Spirit is incarnational: When He comes, He expresses himself in ways that are accessible and understandable to the hearers.

Mike Bickle, in his wonderfully practical book *Growing in the Prophetic,* urges us to not impose dramatic "packaging" over the message the Holy Spirit is bringing.

> For the most part, the same New Testament prophetic gift can operate in very different packages. Usually people have no problem with the woman in the prayer group who feels a burden to pray for someone, who senses the Holy Spirit leading her in prayer, and who states that God is "impressing" something on her heart. All of this is in a package most people are familiar with and understand.
>
> But if she speaks up during the Sunday morning service in her church and loudly proclaims her revelation interspersed with "This saith the Lord" she could get a significantly different response. Here are the same words and the same message, but delievered in a very different package.
>
> Sometimes I think we are too concerned about the package and not enough about the message.
>
> It bothers me when prophetic people preface everything with "Thus saith the Lord." They may say this because they have heard others do it. Or perhaps it is an attempt to be more dramatic or increase the chance of being heard. Sometimes it may come from an Old Testament understanding of the prophetic. Whatever the case, I think it is important that we encourage people to dial down the drama and mysticism when they proclaim what they feel that God has spoken.[3]

As someone who has had the opportunity to minister in very diverse contexts of the body of Christ, one of my strongest prayers is that we would become more aware that very often a great deal of what separates us is our terminology and religious culture. If we could look deeper than the "package" we all wear and really hear each others' hearts in this and other crucial areas, I believe we would be much closer to the unity Jesus prayed we would have in John 17.

HOW DOES HE SPEAK?

If God indeed is speaking today and desires for us to hear His voice, what are the ways He speaks, and how should we seek to hear Him?

First, I would say that we never should seek an experience but always be seeking the Person of Jesus Christ. When we move into a frantic search for the next spiritual high or the thing that will let us "feel" more, we begin to drift toward emotionalism. Emotions are wonderful. God has them, and He gave them to us to fully enjoy. I believe part of the "abundant life" Jesus promised is the full experience of the emotions the Lord has given us the capacity for. But we are not ever to be ruled by our emotions. We are ruled by the Lord and His voice.

But next, the biggest key to hearing the voice of the Lord is very simple. *Listen.*

Quiet your heart, still your mind and simply say, "Jesus, I am here to love You and to hear from You."

Sometimes His voice will come as a picture, sometimes as a Scripture verse that comes to mind seemingly from "out of the blue," sometimes an "inner impression," a sense of knowing and peace about a decision. Sometimes the Lord speaks through dreams or even more dramatic levels of revelation such as visions, angelic visitations or even His audible voice.

The late Francis Schaeffer was one of the most learned, respected Christian leaders in this century. Early in his ministry, Schaeffer faced a minor crisis. He and his young family needed temporary housing during a transition time, but they had very little money. They needed a "minor miracle" from the Lord. While Francis was praying about this, he said to God, "Where can we live? Lord, please show us." Immediately, in response to his question, he heard an audible voice. It wasn't a voice inside of his mind. It didn't come from another human. He was alone. The voice simply said, "Uncle Harrison's house."

Although the answer was very clear—it was an audible voice—it made no sense. Uncle Harrison had never given the Schaeffer family anything, and they thought it would be very unlikely he would offer his house for them to live in. Yet the voice that spoke to Francis was so startling and direct that he felt he had to obey it. He wrote his uncle, asking him what he planned to do with his house the next year. He was astonished when his uncle replied that he planned to live with his brother the next year and would like to offer his house free of rent to Francis and his family for a year. Francis Schaeffer claims this was the second time God had spoken to him in an audible voice.[4]

NO FEAR!

Western Christians have valued rationalism and analysis to such a point that faith and experience with the Lord is largely head knowledge. But God is requiring a heart relationship, which, as stated earlier, has communication as a central part.

I believe that the flow of communication between the Lord and His people in this generation will dramatically and profoundly increase. It is incumbent upon all Christian leaders to grapple to gain a biblical understanding of the realm of the prophetic. We must do this in order to properly nurture and release the body into the glorious adventure of living in true relationship with the Lord, which includes communicating with Him!

No longer can we as leaders allow fear, past hurts, Western culture or religious cultures to keep us from hearing the voice of the Lord and helping our brothers and sisters to do the same. How different our churches would be if our prayer times and communication with heaven truly became a two-way conversation!

It is imperative for our spiritual health in every area that we have systems of checks and balances in place in our life that help us to interpret what the Lord is saying and rightly apply it. If you are just beginning to hear the Lord speak, it is not likely that the first thing you will hear Him say is to sell all and move to Africa to serve Him. Be committed to these disciplines as part of the process in growing in communication with the Lord. Learn to hear Him:

Through His Word

First and foremost, the written Word of God is the standard and rule against which all of life is measured. It contains a wealth of wisdom for those who meditate upon it and hide it in their hearts. Pursuit of sound doctrine must be a constant quest.

Through church history

I believe we can gain wisdom and perspective from the Lord when we study the lives, doctrines and practices of those faithful forerunners who have gone before us. Studying movements and personalities in church history helps us to grow and avoid the pitfalls that some have fallen into.

Through His leaders

It is imperative that each believer be grounded in a strong believing community and in ongoing, honest, submitted relationships of spiritual covering. In a spiritual community, the kingdom blessings of wisdom are released.

Through His body

Again, the Word tells us that "from him the whole body, joined and held together by every supporting ligament, grows and builds itself up in love, as each part does its work" (Eph. 4:16). Being in committed relationships with other strong believers will help you grow in the Lord and stay on track as you learn to hear His voice.

Through His Spirit

Biblical precedents for hearing the Lord include dreams, visions (inward and open), prophecies, angelic visitations, the audible voice of the Lord and prophetic actions or gestures. In this day the church is learning again to cultivate the eyes and ears of our hearts so that we can truly enter into a communion with the Lord.

FROM RECEIVING TO GIVING

The chief reason the Lord is helping this generation rediscover His voice is because He loves us and longs for us to hear Him. But there are other reasons! He has a message He wants us to share. As we grow in learning the voice of the Lord, we are released into being a vessel of His life to others around us.

One very basic way this can be walked out is as we pray for one another. Do you remember the old song "Whistle While You Work"? Well, our adage should be "Listen While You Pray." When you are praying, either alone or for someone else, listen. Ask the Lord to speak to you. Ask Him to guide your thoughts.

As we recover our hearing, we will see tremendous results in evangelism. No longer will our only impetus for sharing the Lord with others be the principle of evangelism, as good as that is. We will begin to be directed by the Lord to those whose hearts are ripe for Him and given supernatural assistance and guidance while ministering to them. The New Testament is full of dramatic accounts of Jesus and His disciples receiving supernatural information about the people to whom they were ministering that their ministry might be more effective and God's power might be shown. It is no different today.

Take a few minutes now, quiet your heart and ask the Lord to speak to you. Entering into the reality of communicating with the Lord will change your life!

What Now?

For group discussion:

1. Discuss the parallels in human communication to our communication with God. In what ways can we learn about God from the way we communicate with others?

2. Play some instrumental worship music. Choose a theme such as mercy, brokenness or hope, and devote fifteen to twenty minutes to individually listen to the words or picture impressions with which you feel the Holy Spirit prompting you. Afterward, share with each other what you felt.

3. We can hear God speaking through His Word, church history, His leaders, His body and His Spirit. Talk about ways you see this happening around you and also how you (as a group and individuals) have been used to communicate God's purposes to others.

For personal application:

1. How do you most easily picture God? For example, as father, friend, shepherd, judge, provider?

2. The biggest key that I know of in hearing the voice of the Lord is very simple—listen. Quiet your heart, still your mind and simply say, "Jesus, I am here to love You and to hear from You." Afterward, write down the impressions you sensed.

3. Think about a time you felt disappointed or forgotten by God. Compare these feelings with places in the Psalms where David cries out to God.

Global Relevance
and Release

*The next generation will be uniquely
equipped and mobilized for cross-cultural evangelism at home
and abroad.*

The world is shrinking.

I was on a plane recently, headed to Nashville. The man seated next to me was from Pennsylvania. When we landed in Nashville and went to collect our luggage, he introduced me to his girlfriend, who had come to pick him up. She did not live in Nashville but in Los Angeles. We made small talk at the conveyor belt, and within a few moments I discovered that she was close friends with the man who produced my last CD, who is from Houston.

THE SIX DEGREES PRINCIPLE

I call this the "six degrees principle." *Six Degrees of Separation* is a play about a homeless con artist who pretends to be the son of Sidney Poitier, and thereby weaves his way in and out of the lives of several prominent New York City families, stealing from them and conning them in the process. He uses the information he gains about the lives of one victimized family to gain the acceptance and trust of his next unsuspecting but equally gullible set of victims.

The basic and amazing underlying premise of the story is that you and any other human being on the planet are separated by only six relationships. Essentially, you are in relationship with someone who is in relationship with someone who is in relationship with someone, and so on, who is in relationship with Pope John Paul II or Madonna or a butcher in Hong Kong—any two people on the planet are separated by only six relationships. Another way to say it is that any two people on the planet are connected by six relationships.

It is an amazing theory. Network marketing companies build their empires on it.

The fact of the matter is that despite the mind-boggling and somewhat scary population explosion, our equally exploding ability to communicate is making the world much, much smaller.

TECHNOLOGY—THE TIE THAT BINDS

There is an almost instantaneous relay of information all around the world. Comparing our lives today with what life was like one hundred years ago is incredible. Pause for a moment and look around the room you are in and consider what would not have been there a mere century ago. Telephones, computers, cell phones, electric lights, microwaves, air conditioners, fax machines, televisions, VCRs. We are caught up in the midst of the technological revolution. We marvel at it, but we can never truly understand the magnitude of it because we are growing alongside it. It is affecting the way we live. Despite any negative feelings we may have toward the concept of a "global village" or a "world community," the unalterable truth is that humanity is connected in a way like never before.

TELEVISION

Without question, the visual media of television and video have become a cord binding the world together in a global consciousness. This medium has created international celebrities like Madonna and Michael Jackson. It has made Coke a more recognized name than Jesus and forever imprinted images such as Neil Armstrong's first steps on the moon or the Tiananmen Square massacre into our global consciousness. Television and the advertising that accompanies it are creating a global awareness, especially among the young, of fashion, music and cultural trends.

A few years ago I was on a backpacking adventure in the rain forest of Central America. I came into a tiny mountain village where running water was a luxury. I was amazed to find that it was movie night, and the whole village had gathered to watch the latest Hollywood offering just a few months after it had premiered in the States. In many Third World countries there are villages that have no running water, but they have television!

All over the world, the latest Hollywood movies are imported. Their values, or lack thereof, are spread out across television and movie screens for all the world to ingest.

The visual media have become an "opiate for the masses." There is an addictive quality to television and videos. Putting the kids in front of a TV or making them watch a video has become a standard tool for raising them. Constant overt and subliminal messages bombard them, urging them to buy this or that.

COMPUTER AND INTERNET

A significant force that is bringing the world closer together every day is the Internet. It is now very easy to maintain consistent communication and relationship with people on the other side of the world. You can exchange information with them almost at will. International friendships developed online bring humanity one step closer to the "global village." Those not raised in the computer generation may view the Internet as another passing technological fad, but it is not. It is here to stay, and it will dramatically change the way we interact with other people.

There are obvious perils to this technology. It has the power to disseminate any type of information to an enormous audience. There is little, if any, ability to supervise or regulate the Internet. Graphic pornography, homemade bomb kits and cult and occult information can be obtained with ease.

The "Net" does, however, offer tremendous opportunities for the advancement of the kingdom. Prayer groups have been established that have the ability to quickly mobilize intercession and awareness on a global scale. Web sites with up-to-date information on missions endeavors and people groups provide ready access to information. These can mobilize and empower people toward missions projects as never before. Missionaries in remote regions who previously would have needed weeks to communicate with friends and relatives can now quickly keep their support network up to date.

TRAVEL

One hundred years ago it took weeks to get from New York City to London. Today it takes hours. The ease and speed of international travel are bringing the world together in amazing ways.

Consider how much more frequently people travel internationally today. It is not unusual for people today to have been to several different countries, either in an exchange program, for business, on vacation or on a missions outreach. Contrast this with a few generations ago when international travel was rare, reserved for diplomats, explorers and the very wealthy. Last year I took my eighty-year-old grandmother to Israel with me for the Feast of *Shavuot* (Pentecost). Not only was it her first time out of the country, it was her first time on a plane!

CULTURE TRAVELS ON THE TECHNOLOGY HIGHWAY

As technology provides for faster, easier communication, the first thing that is exported—even before goods or services—is culture. Multiculturalism—this buzzword is increasingly manifesting as a reality. The urban centers of America are becoming a stew, rather than melting pot, of ethnic groups from around the world. Once upon a time, migration to the

United States meant an immediate desire to learn the language and quickly assimilate into your new identity as an American. Now ethnic groups are holding on to their distinctives in ever-increasing ways. They work toward maintaining language, culture and religion as well as strong ties with their country of origin. The nations truly have come to America's door, but they have kept the door to home open as well.

One gathering place for the nations is the universities of America, where students from the nations of the world flock by the tens of thousands for a chance to secure a brighter future through education. The classrooms of American universities are one of the greatest untapped mission fields in the world.

OPPORTUNITY IS KNOCKING

The discerning believer will see in this convergence of communications and cultures an incredible opportunity for the gospel.

There are some very interesting similarities between the first-century Roman world, in which the apostle Paul lived, and in our own times of the twenty-first century. In almost every sphere of life one can find similarities between these two eras.

FIRST-CENTURY LIFE—A *KAIROS* MOMENT[1]

The strength of the Roman Empire was in its ability to bind together peoples from the multitude of nations that Rome conquered. As the different nations were conquered they were incorporated into the melting pot of Roman life, but they were allowed to maintain many of the distinctives of their ethnic and cultural origins. The Roman Empire allowed each of the subjugated nations to maintain many of their own unique ways (religious practices and beliefs, cultural practices and traditions). But the empire was also fully committed to enforcing laws that would serve as ties to bind together these very different peoples. These ties consisted of learning the required business language (*lingua franca*) of their day (Greek, and in later years Latin), Roman law as the law of the land and a standard, recognized currency.

In addition to these ties, the Romans also poured large sums of money into public works, entertainment facilities and educational institutions. These investments all powerfully served to provide common experiences for people to develop a sense of homogenity among great diversity. Whether in the public baths, at the amphitheaters, at the universities or at the libraries, people of great diversity would meet each other and relationships would begin to cross the lines of ethnicity, culture and religion, allowing a new identity to become a powerful tie in and of itself...Roman culture.

However, one of greatest single factors uniting the empire was the *system of roads*. The Romans built an extensive system of roads that networked the entire empire together. The roads enabled the common person to travel, allowed for an effective mail system and allowed for quick movements of the army to effectively maintain national security.

TWENTY-FIRST CENTURY LIFE—ANOTHER *KAIROS* MOMENT

As we stand in the twenty-first century, we discover that many of the characteristics predominant in the first-century Roman Empire distinctly characterize the modern world today. However, now these characteristics function in much vaster and technologically superior dimensions than the first century and impact not merely a region of the world but literally the entire globe.

The international melting-pot effect of the Roman Empire is part of the DNA of American life and culture. It is seen in virtually every city of the nation and is vividly stated on our currency with the words *e pluribus unum* ("out of many one"). In capital cities all around the world, not just America, one finds this same international flavor as ethnic communities and sections of cities have become part of the normal landscape of city geography.

As with the Roman Empire, there is also a *lingua franca* today, and it is English, the common language used around the world for business. International laws and policies, established through the United Nations, serve to tie our world together. Economically, the world is connected by the American dollar, and soon all of Europe by the Euro. Television, radio and film have created common experiences through music and screen-play for all peoples to identify with and follow. Food and fashion also serve as global ties that provide international contexts with which people anywhere can identify (McDonald's, Pizza Hut, Levis, Nike and Tommy Hilfiger). Colleges and universities in America and Europe bring together people from many different countries as students live with each other through the course of their study.

Truly more than ever in the minds of the peoples of the earth there is a global consciousness and international awareness unprecedented in the history of mankind.

God ordained for the most effective launching pad and birthing place of Christianity to occur in the setting of the first-century Roman Empire. So too God is preparing us today for an even greater releasing of His message and life for a final End-Time release to the nations of the world. Not only are the pieces in place for this to practically occur through technological channels, but we, the messengers, are being prepared by having an international mind-set and global lifestyle. *God has not just prepared the circumstances for a full release of His message, but He has literally prepared the mouthpieces and mind-sets to be more comfortable with such a task.* Even those who have yet to house the living message of God in their very own lives—God is making them ready.

People are not just doing international activities (such as business and travel), but God is giving many believers international lifestyles.

GLOBALISM REDEFINED—A KINGDOM PARADIGM

So what does all this mean?

God has strategically placed this generation, you and me, in a very specific *kairos.*

This *kairos* moment is ripe for the full release of His witness in the earth. God is making use of this global consciousness that has infiltrated the unsaved world, and He is redeeming it for His purposes. God is now raising up masses of Christians who by virtue of their lifestyles are missionaries.

Some are students, and some are businessmen and businesswomen. Some are athletes. Some are entertainers, and others are traveling vacationers.

Along with the divine equipping of lifestyles, there is something of even greater significance happening. There is a deep passionate cry of the Holy Spirit for the salvation of the nations now being released in the soul of the church. Like a holy infection, a burden for the peoples of the world is touching our hearts. The church is becoming supernaturally infused with a faith that is much larger than our local sphere of geography and relational interaction. God is laying the foundation for a kingdom of God paradigm of Christian living to be released upon the church at large.

Many believers today are literally being gripped with compassion for the unsaved as never before. There is a young generation that is being raised up in the spirit of Joshua with lives of holy abandonment to see the kingdom of God advance no matter where it may lead or what the cost. God is raising up a church that is seeing the very meaning and calling of their lives through the lens of the kingdom of God rather than the lens of so-called Christian culture and expected tradition. There is a pioneer spirit sweeping the body, calling us to come away—out of our comfort zones. This company of pioneers and pilgrims have laid hold of the truth that the message of the gospel is a global message, and only because it is a global message (relevant and applicable for anybody, anyplace, anytime) can it truly be called the gospel.

This new wine of the pioneer spirit is being poured into several new wineskins, including those that mobilize global evangelism and global intercession.

JUST DO IT!

There has been a phenomenal rise of missions agencies and movements in the recent past. Loren Cunningham and the YWAM (Youth With A Mission) movement have produced a generation of missions-savvy leaders spanning the globe in a tremendous network.

Ron Luce and the Teen Mania program have enabled thousands of teenagers in the past few decades to stand for Christ on foreign soil.

While some might debate the efficacy of short-term missions on the communities visited, this type of experience surely has deep impact on the lives of those who go, causing them to be more sensitized to the work of missions and the needs of people groups around the world.

Cross-cultural missions does not necessarily mean *overseas*. Bart Campolo, based in Philadelphia, heads up a program called MissionYear. In this cutting-edge program, Bart recruits young adults to join teams that live and work in inner-city neighborhoods in partnership with strong local churches. Many suburban, white, middle-class kids have no idea what America looks like through the eyes of those in the projects and ghettos of America. As these young people simply live together in the midst of these neighborhoods for a year and experience life from a new perspective, stereotypes on both sides are broken down and understanding awakened that can help to make a difference for years to come.

This mobilization to missions is not just in America! Recently I had the tremendous privilege of ministering at Word of Life in Uppsala, Sweden, where Ulf Ekman is the senior pastor. I was amazed to find that in just ten years their Bible college has had over six thousand students. The outreaches going on through Word of Life in India, Russia, Turkmenistan, Uzbekistan and other areas in the 10/40 Window are amazing. The tremendous excitement over sharing the love of Jesus is causing the Swedish young people to radically re-examine their lives, and, for most of them, to pledge to short-term missions. Many of them accept a long-term call from the Lord.

Eagles' Wings has been blessed to mobilize hundreds to short-term missions endeavors around the world in the past few years, working relationally with our international contacts. We look forward to this aspect of our ministry growing as we join the other wonderful mobilizers who are building bridges of relationship in the nations. Our nine-month internship program has also been a dynamic training ground for those who want to receive discipleship and to minister in outreaches, but who aren't feeling called at the moment to a typical four-year Bible college program.

CALLING DOWN FIRE

Accompanying this sovereign burden for the nations is a call to prepare the way in prayer. The Holy Spirit is awakening a global consciousness for the purposes of God today in the earth. Throughout the earth, wonderful networks of intercessors are springing up. Networks of the networks are even forming. The World Prayer Center in Colorado Springs, Colorado, directed by Chuck Pierce, was established to encourage and track current levels of prayer and intercession all over the world. The World Prayer Center helps missionaries and evangelists work with those efforts already in place.

Reconciliation prayer walks, which combine intercessory prayer with a knowledge of the spiritual history of an area, are increasing all around the world today. Christians travel on these missionary/intercessory trips and go from site to site praying for social, political, ethnic, economic and familial healing and restoration in places that have been ravaged by injustices and evils.

While we will cover more about prayer in the chapter on spiritual warfare, it is important to recognize the global thinking of these missions and intercessory movements. They understand that the Holy Spirit is working all over the world, not just in their particular field of ministry or through their denomination or organization. They value networking as never before, and they really see themselves as part of the whole, rather than focused only on their ministry. The AD 2000 Movement, under the capable direction of Dr. Paul Cedar and AIMS (Association of International Missions Services), piloted by the skillful Howard Foltz, are examples of umbrella organizations who help to tie groups together. This atmosphere of unity and humility is one in which the Holy Spirit can work much more significantly, as it assures Him that Jesus' name is being lifted up and His name is receiving all the glory.

WHERE ARE YOU?

I was a young teenager when Keith Green died, and I attended the memorial concert after his death. I will never forget sitting in the auditorium in Buffalo, New York, as his widow, Melody, shared about Keith's passion for missions that was so increasing in the last years of his life. She and Loren Cunningham shared how they believed the Lord was going to raise up tens of thousands of missionaries to go to the nations. They saw Keith as a grain of wheat, planted deep in the heart of a generation. I was emotionally touched with the sadness of Keith's death, but that night something deep and spiritual was happening in me. Though I did not fully understand it, I felt a strong consecration come to my life. I responded to the altar call to dedicate my life to full-time ministry. I look back on that night as one of the pivotal memorials in my walk with the Lord.

At a recent conference where I was ministering, we were in a time of waiting on the Lord in the midst of worship. A young mother came up to the platform. She approached me, carrying her young son in her arms. She asked if she could share something with the congregation.

She said that in the midst of worship, the Lord had been dealing with her regarding her son's life. She began to realize that, like many parents today, she wanted an easy and good life for her child. Naturally, the tendency of parents is to steer their children toward the things that this world deems as important for success. For most, from earliest childhood pressure is exerted on them to get good grades and excel in school so that they can get into a good college. There is little question of whether or not God is calling them to college; it is simply taken as a given that these children, though believers, will follow the normal pattern of this world.

This young mother, now strong with emotion, then said that the Lord instructed her to take her three-year-old son and place him in my arms, as Hannah did with Samuel when she presented him to Eli the priest at the temple of the Lord. In so doing, she believed she was saying to the Lord that not only was the child dedicated to the Lord in terms of his salvation (as is often emphasized at baby dedications), but that whatever service—whatever calling—in the house of the Lord and the kingdom of God was over this young man's life, she was willing to trust him to the Lord. She would not place on him expectations according to the standards of this world system or its thinking or urge him toward whatever security this world can provide. She would truly give him to God, trusting the Lord with his life.

For your life personally, and for the lives of those you influence, how are you responding to the urgency of the hour? Who will be the Jim Elliots, the Keith Greens, the Mother Theresas of today? Will you sell all...? Perhaps the Lord will not require you to sell all outwardly, but He may. But one way or another, He is looking for hearts blazing with fire to go forth in this amazing new *kairos* world that is so much like the *kairos* world of Paul's day! If it is to the heart of Philadelphia or the heart of India, God is looking for those whose security and calling are not anchored in this world and its systems, but anchored in the eternal kingdom. It honestly does not matter if you are seventeen or seventy-one—Jesus commands us to go. (See Matthew 28:18–20.) The nations, either across the ocean or across town, are waiting.

What Now?

For group discussion:

1. How much does your group know or have relationship with the missionaries it supports around the world? What are some ways to increase the consistency of those relationships?

2. What technology is your group currently using to reach out to the lost? In what ways could your group utilize modern technology to reach out to more people?

3. Where are there opportunities in your region to reach out cross culturally? What people groups are represented in your immediate region? Are they represented in your church? How can you reach out to them?

For personal application:

1. How does technology affect you in your daily life? Decide to take one day and live it without modern communications technology—no TV, phone, e-mail or beepers.

2. Consider how technology can actually hinder relationships. How can you keep that from happening?

3. Do you have any relationships outside of your own ethnic background? Be intentional about growing in friendship with someone from a different background than your own.

4

~

Living Stones

*The next generation will be
relationally driven.*

The following is an excerpt from a book for children called *Alone After School.* It is described as a "self-care guide for latchkey children."

> This chapter will teach you many ways of knowing whether or not you are sick enough to need to call a doctor. Also, it will teach you how to carefully pick the time to talk with your parents. It is important for you to remember that parents are usually exhausted when they first come home from work. You will also make some lists, including "Things I can do when I am Lonely" and "Things I can do when I am Scared."[1]

America is paying an incredible price for its worship of the ancient gods of greed, status and materialism. The nation is whirling about at a dizzying pace, running around with a crazed need for validation from "the Joneses." But somehow we are oblivious to the emotional, moral and spiritual vacuum being created by this insanity. We are so busy making a living that we have forgotten what it means to have a life. Our society is like a person whose clothing has caught on fire and who is refusing to "stop, drop and roll." We continue to run around trying to deal with the problem, though our actions only serve to increase it.

The result is a generation left without a context for healthy growth. In the past, if there were a breakdown in the nuclear family, there would be other healthy contexts offered by society for an individual to find a sense of place, purpose and personhood. Now, I believe most in this generation view any institution with utter suspicion and would rather rely on their relational tribe to help see one another through.

F Is for Failure

Institutional contexts of trust have disappeared from our societal landscape. Let's consider some of them.

Family
The statistics are so well known and often repeated that it seems redundant to raise them again. Unfortunately, American churches continue to operate programs from assumptions that presuppose a healthy traditional nuclear family in America, which is at best a minority and quickly becoming almost mythic.

- Cohabitation has risen by more than 500 percent in the past two decades.
- One out of three children born this year will be born to an unwed mother.
- Less than half of all children live in their biological nuclear family.[2]

American sitcoms used to center around the traditional family—*Leave It to Beaver, The Waltons, Little House on the Prairie.* They have given way to shows like *Party of Five,* a show about five siblings raising themselves without parents; *Ellen,* where the main character comes to terms with her lesbianism; *Friends* and *Seinfeld,* both demonstrating people's primary emotional support context to be whatever friendships they can make and manage to hold on to.

Education

The American educational system used to be the best in the world. It was a context that could offer personal growth and the impartation of not only knowledge but also life values. It has now become an untended smorgasbord of junk food. George Barna, in his vital book *The Second Coming of the Church,* offers these alarming statistics from a United States Department of Education study.

- Forty-six percent of American adults are either functionally or marginally illiterate.
- More than one million of last year's high school graduates received their diplomas even though they could not read and write at an eighth-grade level.[3]

Beyond the obvious problems of what schools are not providing in way of education are the terrifying problems that are a part of the schools of America. Teenagers must wade through a daily battle of drugs, violence and promiscuity, all in an atmosphere of moral relativism. Consider the following chart, which compares the top disciplinary problems in 1940 and 1992.

TOP DISCIPLINARY PROBLEMS
ACCORDING TO PUBLIC SCHOOL TEACHERS

1940	1992
1. Talking out of turn	1. Drug abuse
2. Chewing gum	2. Alcohol abuse
3. Making noise	3. Pregnancy
4. Running in the halls	4. Suicide
5. Cutting in line	5. Rape

6. Dress-code violations

7. Littering

6. Robbery

7. Assault [4]

Government

There was a day in this country when there was a sense of pride in being an American. Our flag, our history, our standards meant something. Though we were of varied backgrounds and ethnicities, we were Americans and had a genuine sense of unity and national identity. Civic and political awareness and involvement were viewed as positive goals and interests.

Today the scandals and endless debates from Washington all the way to local politics have jaded our trust. We don't believe in America any more because we don't know who we are, where we have come from or where we are going. Politicians are immediately viewed with suspicion. We have come a long way from the ideals of *Mr. Smith Goes to Washington.*

America's response to the Clinton presidency shows that we don't expect honesty and integrity from our officials because we don't believe in those ideals any longer. Our attitude has turned from outrage to frustration to tolerance to resignation and acceptance. Since we no longer expect integrity, we look for results, and invariably those results are measured in dollar signs. Economic stability has become the only thing we seem to care about.

Church

One of society's greatest disappointments has been us, the church. We have not been salt. We have not been light. We have trumpeted an uncertain sound. We judge the world in the spirit of the Pharisee while forgetting that judgment begins with us, the house of God.

George Barna, one of the most learned and balanced commentators on the church in America, has this to say:

> At the risk of sounding like an alarmist, I believe the Church in America has no more than five years—perhaps even less—to turn itself around and begin to affect the culture, rather than be affected

by it…The downfall of the Church has not been the content of its message but its failure to practice those truths. Those who have turned to the Church seeking truth and meaning have left empty-handed, confused by the apparent inability of Christians to implement the principles they profess… *The systems, structures, institutions and relational networks developed for the further-ance of the Church are archaic, inefficient, ineffective—and perhaps, even unbiblical.*[5]

The sad and highly televised ministry scandals of the late eighties were no doubt harmful to the world's view of the church. Certainly, though, they were not the only thing that caused us to lose validity in the eyes of the world. Moral failure and ministry burnout has been rampant among clergy at a local level. We can shake our heads in frustration, or we can ask the hard question. What is wrong with our church system that so many good men and women in ministry fall? Without denying individual responsibility for sin, we must ask ourselves why these problems are so systemic. Otherwise we will simply go on perpetrating a church culture that allows for more of the same.

Hypocrisy is one reason the church has failed in the world's eyes. Irrelevance is another. How relevant are we? I appreciate the sincerity of those involved in Christian television ministry and believe strongly that there is a place for Christian programming. However, I often shudder when I consider what kind of impression the average American gets while channel surfing and happening across some Christian TV.

TRIBAL DRUMS ARE BEATING

The loss of health in the above contexts, and in society as a whole, has left a generation not knowing where they can grow up. Since they can't trust the people and systems that were supposed to nurture them, they have decided to trust each other.

This is resulting in an increase of tribalism evidenced in all different forms. The Nation of Islam with Louis Farrakhan, the skinhead neo-Nazi movement, the gay movement, the fantasy role-playing game movement. In music, it is the grunge movement, the rap movement and the Goth movement. These are not just styles of music; they have become a way of life. The singers and artists are not just performers anymore. They are the prophets of their generation—the elders—the leaders, holding the tribe together through the glue of music, clothing style and other paraphernalia. MTV broadcasts the message all over the world. In effect a TV channel has become the new after-school clubhouse where kids hang out and subconsciously gain their value system, or lack thereof. Listen to their skepticism in the following description of Generation X.

WE ARE GENERATION X

We are...the lost generation. Sociologists call us...Generation X, Baby Busters, Thirteeners.

We were born between 1961 and 1980...
Too late for the American dream.

We are...tired of talk with little action or results.

We are...tired of symbols and flowery talk. Just get to the point.

We are...so sick of the bureaucracy, that instead of trying to change things we just figure...Why bother?

We are...not too happy with the "baby boomer" generation of our parents, to say the least.

We've seen how "if it feels good, do it" has broken our homes...

And our hearts...

It has exploded the American deficit and screwed us out of the American Dream.

We are... tired of boomers acting like money and success is it, while sacrificing us, their children, and their fellow man.

They talk of making the world a better place while ignoring their families.

If "all you need is love," then we'd like to know where it's all gone...

We are... tired of seeing churches where there's a lot of talk of love but very little shown. There's talk of helping the world, but the churches seem to be full of bickering, rhetoric, greed, and self-centeredness.

We know we need God badly, but we have a hard time trusting anyone to tell us where to find Him.

We can know God. He wants to know us badly.[6]

The failure of family, government, education and church has left a void, and that void is being filled by these tribes. *If the church does not make the transition from organized institution to organic tribe—a living community—we will lose the next generation and pay the price for it in complete societal breakdown and eventual anarchy.* If compassion for the lost and obedience to the Great Commission are not enough to motivate us to radical action, perhaps fear of societal chaos and personal loss will.

We have an entire generation that needs to be parented! Parenting cannot take place in ninety minutes on a Sunday morning or at a Friday night youth group with a youth pastor who stays an average of 1.2 years per church. The church must become a living community—a place of honesty, safety, healing and depth.

A word of reality to those who would flippantly and light-heartedly compare this day and age to the sixties counterculture movement and see it simply as a passing adolescent phase. You are wrong.

The sixties were about dropping out and tuning in. This generation is just about about dropping out, because there is nothing to tune in to. The sixties were about "giving peace a chance," flower power and love. Today's generation has a dark, nihilistic, self-destructive wound at its heart. This generation is waiting for destruction and believes love is an illusion because everyone who was supposed to love them has failed them—especially their fathers.

COME ON, ELIJAH!

> See, I will send you the prophet Elijah before that great and dreadful day of the LORD comes. He will turn the hearts of the fathers to their children, and the hearts of the children to their fathers; or else I will come and strike the land with a curse.
>
> —MALACHI 4:5–6

Fatherlessness certainly will bring a curse. Our nation is bearing the fruit of fatherlessness in a myriad of ways. We all know it! We know the statistics, and inherently we know that the root of societal problems is the breakdown of the family. And the breakdown of the family is largely due to the absent, abusive or withdrawn father.

Floyd McClung, in his pioneering book *The Father Heart of God*, underscores this point.

> Our world is plagued by an epidemic of pain. With divorce rampant and child abuse screaming from the national headlines, it is not surprising that for many people the concept of Father God evokes responses of anger, resentment and rejection. Because they have not known a kind, caring, earthly father, they have a distorted view of the Father's love. In many cases these hurting individuals choose to simply deny or ignore His existence.[7]

Oftentimes even Christian fathers who outwardly do the right things struggle desperately with feelings of inadequacy, loneliness and fear of intimacy, even with their wives and children. They seem unable to break out of the stereotype that society and their own pasts have placed upon them. They simply cannot share deeply with their families or lead them effectively in spiritual growth. Usually these men had the same emotional distance between them and their fathers, and they don't know how to be any different.

But they will be different. They will face their fears by God's grace and open their hearts to receive healing and cleansing. Then they will open their arms to embrace their hurting families, churches and communities. They will because they must. The secret to America's healing is for our Father to heal fathers, who then will heal the sons and daughters.

Sovereignly, the power of God is healing the hearts of His people. In a massive move, He is beginning by healing the hearts of men, so men can become the agents of blessing God has called them to be in their families, churches and communities. The Father's heart for men, a heart of compassion, love, faithfulness and mercy, is being experienced as never before. It is happening in the midst of the renewal services sweeping the nations. It is happening in the joy of brotherhood being experienced by the Promise Keepers. Something is unlocking the hearts of men, cleansing their wounds and releasing them into greater authentic authority.

WERE YOU AT THE MALL?

The thing I will always remember about the Promise Keepers "Stand in the Gap" gathering was the holy silence. As Jack Hayford, Joseph Garlington and others led us through the day, there were regular times of repentance and prayer where all million-plus of us were invited to get on our knees and pray. Each time we did, I was astounded that we were surrounded by absolute silence. How could there be total silence in the midst of a million people in the center of Washington, D.C.? But there was—a holy silence that spoke volumes of the history being made that day in heaven and earth.

I believe the Promise Keepers movement, and especially that day, are a sign and a wonder for us. The power of God's Spirit moved on the men as priests of this nation to come in humble penitence and ask the Father's forgiveness. As fathers' hearts are healed by Father's love, these men begin to walk in healthy, healed relationships with other men, sometimes for the first time in their lives. These healed relationships become sources of healing that begin to spread through local churches.

STONE UPON STONE

Invariably, questions rise about the models and leadership systems in place that sufficed during unhealthy times, but seem constricting to a healthy church life.

The kingdom of God is built together like a "spiritual house" of "living stones" (1 Pet. 2:4–5). It is a relational kingdom—relationship with God, with one another and with the world. It is vital that we come to a clearer understanding of what it means to walk in healthy relationships. They are the context God has ordained for our growth.

> As iron sharpens iron, so one man sharpens another.
> —PROVERBS 27:17

> Speaking the truth in love, [we] may grow in all things into Him who is the head—Christ—from whom the whole body, joined and knit together by what every joint supplies, according to the effective working by which every part does its share, causes growth of the body for the edifying of itself in love.
> —EPHESIANS 4:15–16, NKJV

God has called us together as a body—cells in a body if you will—working in harmony and unity with the Holy Spirit and one another. (See 1 Corinthians 12.) None of us live in a vacuum. Our actions or lack of action will affect the rest of the whole. The only cells that are independent from the rest of the body are either dead or diseased.

We are discussing the concept of authentic relationship. Perhaps you are wondering what I mean by authentic relationship. How can we gauge if we are moving in healthy relationships within the body of Christ? What are some signs of authentic relationship?

It is interesting that in Europe the word *friend* is used much more selectively than here in the United States. A person is generally introduced as an *acquaintance,* sometimes for years, before the term *friend* is applied to the relationship. What a contrast to America, where the term *friend* is used so loosely.

The following is a list of some characteristics of relationships that are authentic—real. It is by no means exhaustive, and certainly emphasizing one characteristic too much can be a sign of an *unhealthy* relationship. But as we consider these indicators, ask yourself, Do I have relationships, outside of family, that meet several or most of these criteria? If so, how many of these relationships do I have?

AUTHENTIC RELATIONSHIPS

- Authentic relationships have *regular interaction.*

Each of us has dear old friends whom we only see or talk to once or twice a year—an old college roommate, the maid of honor from your wedding. There is precious, poignant, sentimental value to these relationships. Precious though they are, they do not provide the kind of regular involvement that "iron sharpening iron" calls for.

Authentic relationships must have some kind of regular interaction. In today's world of technology and travel, these may not be people in your neighborhood, but they must be people who interact with you enough to "track" with your life. They need to be familiar with your ups and downs, your joys and struggles. Only then will they have enough history to discern patterns and speak into your life situation with a sense of history and context.

- Authentic relationships have some *length of relationship.*

It is easy in our microwave society to meet people, impress them with our personality and drift into short-term friendships. These types of relationships, however, don't stand the test of time. It's easy to quickly feel close to someone and be thrilled that you may have found a true friend. Many times, though, these relationships falter as quickly as they grew, even if some deep communication was shared. The seeds of authentic relationship were planted, but they did not take root. All of us have these types of relationships, and they are a right and normal part of the human experience.

However, in the midst of this, there should be some relationships that endure the ups and downs, job transfers, life changes and so on, while still maintaining depth and not becoming the more sentimental relationships described above. There should be a select few people with whom you are intentionally building a history.

- Authentic relationships *admit weaknesses.*

Each of us attempts to show ourselves in our best light, to "put our best foot forward" and make a good first impression. There is nothing wrong with this. But at some point, we must have a cluster of people, other than just our family, with whom we share our shortcomings and weaknesses.

Consider Paul, the strong apostle, baring his heart in vulnerability to his faithful friend, Timothy.

> Do your best to come to me quickly, for Demas, because he loved this world, has deserted me and has gone to Thessalonica. Crescens has gone to Galatia, and Titus to Dalmatia. Only Luke is with me....Alexander the metalworker did me a great deal of harm....At my first defense, no one came to my support, but everyone deserted me.
>
> —2 Timothy 4:9–11, 14, 16

It does not take much to hear Paul's cry to Timothy here. "Timothy, I am lonely! I know I have preached wonderful messages and had wonderful revelations of divine mysteries! Right now, though, people have hurt me and deserted me. I am a human being who is lonely, and I need you, young friend."

So much in our culture flies in the face of the admission of weakness. The strong, we are told, hold it all in and keep going on. Authentic friendships provide safe contexts to destroy that lie.

• Authentic relationships *share hopes and dreams.*

So many times, bottled up inside of us, are hopes and dreams we are afraid to share with anyone for fear of being perceived as foolish or silly. We would rather keep our dream to ourselves rather than risk the chuckle or even ridicule of another.

Authentic relationships break through this barrier and provide a safe place for us to become dreamers again!

Each year, Eagles' Wings sponsors the East Coast Leadership Conference. The conference is specifically targeted to bless and impact the church on the East Coast, but it has drawn thousands of believers from around America and as many as fifteen nations. It has become one of the key annual gathering times for believers to receive vital ministry. The birth of this conference evidences the above point.

I was living in Jerusalem, Israel, when one day in prayer I had an inner picture of Boston, New York City, Philadelphia, Baltimore and Washington, D.C. I saw all five of these cities as though I were hundreds of miles high looking down on them. Each of them had fire within and around them. I asked the Lord what I was seeing, and I sensed His voice telling me that He was going to send the fire of His glory to these cities. It was then, almost in a moment, that the vision of the East Coast Leadership Conference was downloaded to my spirit. I sensed that part of His strategy, part of the way He would begin to send His glory, was through these conferences. The only problem was that I was twenty-two years old, and Eagles' Wings at that time was me and a post office box! How was I to accomplish this tremendous vision?

Two authentic relationships deeply encouraged me at this time. Rick and Patti Ridings are anointed intercessory leaders in the body of Christ who are known around the world. They are dear friends of mine, and they patiently listened to me around their kitchen table a few weeks later as I shared this vision. Rather than discounting it or telling me how it couldn't be done, Rick encouraged me with some practical steps I could take. He told me to trust that if this truly was a vision from the Lord, then He would bless the endeavor.

As a result of Rick's encouragement, one of the first steps I took was to write to Mike Bickle. I had known Mike for a few years at that point, and I asked him to pray about this vision. If he felt good about the conference, I asked if he would get behind the vision of the conference in practical ways.

I still have the letter Mike sent me, assuring me of his support, but making sure I understood the enormity of what I was undertaking. He affirmed to me that even if the conference never came to be, he was proud of me for endeavoring to obey God and walk in this big dream. Years later, this conference has been a great blessing to literally thousands of people because my friends listened to the vision and encouraged me! What a foundation this has laid for further "faith-risk" steps in my life as the Lord continues to speak! How many dreams are lost because people are too scared to share them? Dreams need the water of encouragement to take root and grow!

- Authentic relationships *question each other about misunderstandings.*

One of the true tests of the authenticity and quality of our relationships is our actions when misunderstandings arise. Generally, human beings avoid confrontation. Our natural tendency is to either a) pretend we are not really bothered by the situation, or b) harbor a secret offense against the other party. In either case, we have begun to build a wall, weakening the unity of the body of Christ and hindering God's blessing upon us. Offenses, even seemingly small ones that we think we can handle, are a serious matter. Offenses breed like a cancer under the superficial surface of religious smiles. Offense grows deep in the soul, sending down roots of bitterness. Outwardly it can go undetected for years. But, like cancer, there will be symptoms that settle in the body. A fatigue, a general sense of things "not being right" will fill the atmosphere.

We must have relationships in which we quickly and lovingly deal with any misunderstandings or misperceptions. Many times, there will not be any real problem—simply a difference in communication style. Sometimes raising an issue will be the first step toward a deeper, more serious problem finally coming to light. In any event, we must overcome the fear of man and our comfort zone that makes us want to "leave well enough alone." We must deal in love with one another. If real relational problems and difficulties occur, then agree on an objective third party who can be a peacemaker and help search out the truth of a matter. If we are more committed to walking in truth than being right, we are already on the road to victory.

It is interesting to note the level of openness in Jesus' relationships with Mary, Martha and Lazarus. We can first notice it in the famous scene with Mary sitting at Jesus feet.

> But Martha was distracted by all the preparations that had to be made. She came to him and asked, "Lord, don't you care that my sister has left me to do all the work by myself? Tell her to help me!"
> —LUKE 10:40

We normally interpret this as an expression of Martha's indignation with Mary, and certainly that was there. But take notice at whom the accusation was directed: "Lord, do *You* not care?

Martha and Jesus had an authentic enough relationship that she could express her frustration at His seeming lack of concern. Jesus replies appropriately, giving a wonderful example of how we should speak the truth in love. "Martha, Martha…you are worried and upset about many things" (Luke 10:41). "I affirm, Martha, that this is your perception and how you are feeling based upon your circumstances. I love you enough to see the situation from your perspective. *But only one thing is needed.* However, I love you enough not to commiserate with you in your offense or let you stay in a mind-set that is self-centered and ultimately self-destructive. I will tell you the truth, though it is painful for you to hear, because we are in authentic relationship and I love you."

We can see the same pattern repeated in John 11 in the dialogue surrounding Lazarus's death. Martha comes to Jesus, in the midst of her grief, with the sense of betrayal that Jesus had not been there in her family's moment of need (v. 21). Mary, even more demonstratively, shares her sense of disappointment in Jesus (v. 32). Of course, we all know the story of Lazarus's resurrection, but an interesting note here in reference to our discussion is the level of honest communication evidenced in Jesus' close relationships.

- Authentic relationships *genuinely desire the success of the other individual and are willing to sacrifice toward that end.*

Kingdom relationships are not based on earthly measurements or thinking. Rather, our goal is to assist each other in discovering God's destiny for our lives and then committing ourselves to see that destiny fulfilled. We recognize that when one member of the body excels and is blessed, we are all strengthened, and so we are not insecure or jealous based on outward factors.

I don't know what relationship shows this more powerfully to us in Scripture than that of David and Jonathan. Jonathan's father, Saul, had forfeited his right to the throne of Israel by his stubborn, unyielded heart. Though he retained the position, it was clear that the anointing was upon David, as David increased in fame, might and blessing. In the midst of this, Jonathan and David had a deep, authentic, covenant relationship.

Jonathan, rather than trying to maintain his own status or position, rightly discerned the will of the Lord in the situation. He clearly pledged his loyalty to David's success, even though it would probably mean his own decrease.

> While David was at Horesh in the Desert of Ziph, he learned that
> Saul had come out to take his life. And Saul's son Jonathan went to

David at Horesh and helped him find strength in God. "Don't be
afraid," he said. "My father Saul will not lay a hand on you. You will
be king over Israel, and I will be second to you. Even my father Saul
knows this."

—1 SAMUEL 23:15–17

Jonathan correctly understood the will of the Lord in regard to his
friend. He sacrificed his own interests to see God's will accomplished in
David's life. If we were in Jonathan's place, how many of us would have
been tempted to try and find a way to help our friend but still cover our
own interests? I'm afraid if I were Jonathan, the conversation may have
gone something like this.

"David, it's obvious God is with you. Let's find a way for you and I to
work this out peacefully—after all, we are great friends! Why don't your
men help me overthrow my father? Then when I am king, I will install you
as commander of my armies! We could even divide the kingdom up and
give you areas to rule in!"

How easy it is for us to try to fit our own interests into God's plans! We
are insecure in God's love for us apart from outward standards of success. We are unable to trust that He has our own best interests at heart. As
a result, we muddy the waters of God's river of purpose with our own
agendas and ideas.

- Authentic relationships allow for *honesty about past hurts and
  confession of sin.*

> Confess your faults one to another, and pray one for another, that ye
> may be healed.
>
> — JAMES 5:16, KJV

Our primary weapon in spiritual warfare is light. The enemy dwells in
darkness—things that are hidden and covered. As things are exposed, be
they wounds or sins, they lose their power.

Intentionally bringing issues out into the light in relationships is one of the most powerful and liberating things we can do in our walk with God. This does not mean we unwisely share areas of struggle, shame or pain with just anyone. But it does mean that a sign of personal health is having some relationships where there is real accountability. Difficult questions about hurts and temptations can be asked and the freedom of Christ ministered in power between one another.

- Authentic relationships *exchange appropriate affection.*

Some may be surprised at the inclusion of this indicator and view it as nonessential. However, let us look at some biblical precedents and cultural needs that make it an important point.

I will never forget being with a tour group a few years ago in Israel. I was with a church from the South. I was taking them around, showing them the sites. We were walking down Ben Yehuda street, an area filled with outdoor cafés, shops, artists and the like. As we were walking around enjoying the sites, one of the very proper ladies in the group came up to me and said, "I can't believe how many homosexuals there are here!"

I said, "Why do you say that?"

"Look at them," she said. "They are so open about it!" She pointed to several pairs of women and pairs of men walking arm and arm.

I laughed and explained to her that it is common for women and even men in Middle Eastern cultures to walk arm in arm, embrace and kiss on the cheek as a way of greeting. She listened to my explanation but still seemed pretty suspicious!

We see evidence of human emotions being displayed through appropriate physical affection throughout Scripture. In one of the most poignant moments of great pain in David and Jonathan's relationship, the Scripture gives us this picture.

> David got up from the south side of the stone and bowed down before Jonathan three times, with his face to the ground. Then they kissed each other and wept together—but David wept the most.
>
> —1 Samuel 20:41

The New Testament records how John, the disciple whom Jesus loved, leaned on Jesus' breast at the Last Supper. This gesture was culturally normative, but it still indicated the true, intimate friendship they shared. (See John 13:23, 25.)

I raise this point because oftentimes we dismiss things by saying they are not culturally normative for us, without questioning if that is a healthy aspect of our culture. For sure, Western civilization is less comfortable with many of these outward displays of affection. But if we are to become the relational family God has called us to be to heal a hurting world, we are going to receive into our midst a huge number of people who have never known appropriate physical affection. For many today, most, if not all, of the physical contact they have ever known has come in the way of violence or sexual abuse. The physical abuse leaves emotional scars that need to be healed through avenues of prayer and counseling. Part of that healing process can come when wounded people begin to receive appropriate physical expressions of love and affirmation, some for the first time. Don't allow our cultural norm of restraint keep us from giving a touch of healing and encouragement.

- Authentic relationships *balance relationship and function.*

There is a constant tension in relationships between whether the relationship is simply for the relationship's sake, or whether it is held together by some common goal, such as a specific ministry or project.

Truly, all healthy relationships should eventually go beyond themselves in imparting life to others. A married couple eventually pour their love into their children. If childless, they pour into those causes and people they can help. Relationships that exist solely for the enjoyment of the relationship are ingrown and can become unhealthy and idolatrous.

At the same time, if all that is driving a relationship is a purpose or goal, then each party will have a hard time really trusting and giving themselves to the relationship. The forwarding of the agenda will be seen as primary, and function becomes valued over personhood. People will feel in this scenario that they constantly need to "perform" properly or they may be discarded from the relationship. This foundation is too shaky for lasting authenticity.

As with many things, the truth here is a paradox. We must hold together two seemingly opposing truths and find health in the center of the two. People are to be valued just for who they are, not for what they do or what they provide for us or our church, ministry or business. This counteracts the tendency toward a performance mentality where worth is based on productivity. On the other hand, the kingdom of God is about bearing fruit, and people who are maturing in Christ should be "value-added" blessings to their communities of faith. This counteracts a tendency toward codependency, where a relationship is based on need rather than health.

MORE EFFECTIVE WINESKINS

Individual healing and relational healing have resulted in leadership structures across the nation that I believe are wonderful indicators of where we are heading. There are several different movements and trends that the body of Christ is embracing right now as we look for more effective wineskins and leadership styles. Let me say that I believe they are all a response to the graciousness of the Lord, who is pouring out a fresh invitation to accept the healing of His Father's love. From this new place of health, He is sending us to be instruments of that healing to a broken, bleeding church and world.

The world, including the church, is full of hurting people, many whom have never had a healthy context for personal growth and healing. The natural tendency of hurting people is to keep walls of self-defense in place. *Unfortunately, most of our church structures accommodate those walls.* There is very little opportunity for trust to develop, for people to open up about their hurts or their past, or for people to develop meaningful, life-giving relationships. If it happens, it is a divine accident rather than an intentional goal. And those who do develop healthy, life-giving relationships within the context of the local church are generally those people who would blossom in whatever context they found themselves. If you are blessed to have healthy relationships in your church, thank God for them! However, that is not necessarily evidence that you are providing an intentional structure where broken people can grow.

Another negative result of these inefficient church structures is that when people *do* need to open up, or their situations become desperate enough, the focus is all on one person—the pastor. So the emotional crises of two or three hundred people are placed on one individual's shoulders. Is it any wonder that pastors burn out?

Paramount to the local church's mission must be the development of structures that anticipate, encourage and at some level, require *intentional relational development* within the body. This type of structure provides the climate of safety where people's defenses can come down. Then their hearts can be ministered to and true growth can take place.

Integral to the relational structure is the identifying, equipping and releasing of the saints to do the work of the ministry. This is in direct opposition to the corporate structure in place in most American churches, where we hire specialists to handle departments. It is a well-known fact that in most American churches, the total ministry and life of the church is carried on by 15 percent of the congregation. The other 85 percent come for the show. It goes something like this.

Churches hire a dynamic (hopefully) individual, the pastor, who needs to have enough charisma to keep a handful of department heads on board. He does this either through hiring them or keeping volunteers happy. This small group of five or so then needs to mobilize the remaining 15 percent from the congregation so that the programs can be offered for the 85 percent who are essentially only interested in the show. What the pastor and his 15 percent produce is based on program and does not demand, in any measurable way, true discipleship. Why, then, are we confused and frustrated when we have attenders and audiences rather than healthy, reproducing disciples? We are getting exactly what we are advertising for!

To radically begin the implementation of wineskins and structures that inherently require accountability and growth will upset the apple cart.

People may leave. But the joy of walking with seventy-five committed believers in true community cannot be compared to the drudgery of maintaining something already dead. And now pruned of the dead branches, that tree of seventy-five is stronger to support an influx of teachable hearts and raise up a mature body.

Let's examine some new structures that are facilitating this kind of life. We will look at several trends and structures, but the underlying message is the same. *As God calls His body to intimate relationship with His Son, we are naturally being drawn to more authentic relationships with one another.* As we look at these structures, it is imperative to realize that these structures will be just as lifeless and ineffective as those we have walked in if they are not fueled with honesty, humility, brokenness, transparency, repentance and an admission of our personal weakness. The time has come for the body of Christ, from the leadership down, to turn from competition to cooperation; from suspicion to trust; from walls to doors; from separatism to communion.

Thankfully, this is happening. Though it may be the "cloud as small as a man's hand," there is evidence of Elijah's "heart turning" at work (1 Kings 18:44).

FROM CELLS TO CELLS

Probably the most effective *lifestyle* that churches are embracing today to move toward relational Christianity is the cell model. Before we go on, let me speak to those of you who are tempted to skip this section.

I urge those of you who may have tried cell groups in the past and found they "just didn't work" for you to read the above sentence again.

Do you notice the word *lifestyle?*

Cell groups or small groups will not work if they are a program or experiment. They must be embraced as a lifestyle change for a church. Doing this will affect everything else about that church. Other things in church life will have to be altered, modified and even sacrificed for the transition to be real and complete. But evidence shows that the prize is well worth the cost.

Larry Kreider is the international director of DOVE Christian Fellowship, a network of cell-based churches around the world. He has been one of the foremost international leaders in the burgeoning cell church movement. His book *House to House* is a standard for those desiring a clear understanding of this movement. Kreider quotes James Rutz and gives some interesting history on when the church may have first become known as a building rather than a living community.

> It was 323 A.D., almost three hundred years after the birth of the church, that Christians first met in something we now call a "church building." For all three hundred years before that, the church met in living rooms!
>
> Constantine built these assembly buildings for Christians not only in Constantinople, but also in Rome, Jerusalem and many parts of Italy, all between 323 and 327. This then triggered a massive church building "fad" in large cities all over the Empire.[8]

Kreider, one of the most humble and effective leaders of the church in this hour, shares plainly from twenty years of international ministry on the essence of the cell movement.

> Today's church has tried to reach people for Christ in our communities with extravagant church programs and 20th century methodology. While such methods have their place, they can never substitute for personal relationships formed in the context of genuine Christian community.
>
> Our cell groups are not simply a program of the church; they are the place where people have the chance to experience and demonstrate New Testament Christianity built on relationships, not simply meetings. In cell groups, people share their lives together and reach out with the healing love of Jesus to a broken world.[9]

I love DOVE's vision statement.

Our Vision
To build a relationship
With Jesus,
With one another,
And to reach the world from
House to house
City to city
Nation to nation.[10]

True relationship with God, true relationship with people. It's what Christianity is all about. *It's what this world is starving for.*

Ralph Neighbour, an authority on the cell church movement, offers seven key reasons why the biblical cell model is so effective. He delineates these in detail in his book *Where Do We Go From Here?*, but I will simply offer them as highlights.

1. *Cell churches are more efficient than traditional churches.* They utilize a much higher percentage of members than the standard 15 percent, because the focus becomes the raising up of leaders.

2. *Cell churches are based on the scriptural concept of community.*

3. *Cell churches maintain a high priority on prayer.*

4. *Cell churches penetrate deeply into the structures of the city* because they reach people relationally in the home and in the marketplace, instead of in a church building where an unbeliever has his defenses up.

5. *The cell church model is more in keeping with the history of the church as a movement.*

6. *The cell church is not limited by the size of a building or the concept of one senior pastor.*

7. *The cell church allows unbelievers to see the work of God in our midst rather than simply hearing a salvation message.*[11]

Larry Kreider's *House to House* and Ralph Neighbour's *Where Do We Go From Here?* are excellent resources that I highly recommend for a more thorough treatment of this trend.

FROM WALL STREET
TO YANKEE STADIUM

Another massive shift coming out of relational Christianity is the trend toward *team ministry*. The day of the superstar ministry has ended. I fully believe that God is requiring all of us, no matter how dynamic or anointed we may think we are, to function as a part of a team.

Unfortunately, most local churches have a corporate America, CEO model of leadership, where the pastor is paid to think, pray, hear God and lead. Board meetings or elderships meetings are too often a time to ratify what the pastor has already decided rather than opportunities for the leadership of the local fellowship to grapple together to hear what the Lord is saying.

This not only keeps the people of God from rising up into leadership but places an incredible pressure on the pastor. Truly, God *does* anoint individuals to lead, and the primary direction will generally come from the senior leader. But I believe the confirmation, timing and working out of that direction will often come from the wisdom of the team.

I want to clearly say that I am not bashing pastors! I believe most pastors are sincere, well-meaning individuals who love God and His people and want their lives to make a difference for the kingdom. We have simply adopted the only model of church that we have ever seen! I am saying that all the societal and church evidence, statistically and subjectively, supports the conclusion that something is drastically wrong with the model we are using! Again, I urge us to hear Barna.

A serious problem calls for a serious remedy. The time for commissions and ecumenical debates is past. Merely tinkering with processes and structures will not do. Where a strong dose of medicine may have healed some of our infirmities in the past, we now require major reconstructive surgery if we are to move beyond reliance upon life support systems.[12]

Dan Juster, one of the most brilliant and articulate leaders of our day, chronicles his own brush with burnout in the early days of his ministry brought on by wrong structures.

Beth Messiah was a moderate sized congregation of 125. There were many hurting people. I offered myself to counsel and pastor the people, but was totally unprepared for the amount of counsel, demand, strife, and difficulty that such a group could generate...I was overwhelmed, worn out, and losing the support of my abandoned wife. It was at this point I began to ask other pastors about their lives. Were they happy? How did they handle the pressures? I was amazed at the answers. Actually they were not answers but attempts at evasions.

"We will reap a good reward if we do not grow weary in well doing," they said. "The Lord is good."

"Yes," I protested, "but I did not ask if the Lord was good. I asked if you were happy in pastoral ministry."

I found that most of the pastors I was meeting were unhappy. Their expectations were not fulfilled. They constantly experienced guilt and frustration that they were not meeting the needs of the people. Evangelism was not greatly successful. Most growth was transfer growth from other churches.

These men were putting in long hours from morning till night six or seven days a week. Most people have no idea or empathy for what most pastors go through—the long hours, the disappointments, the betrayals, and the attacks...*The model they are following sets them up for burn out or disillusionment.*[13]

Juster then goes on to chronicle the massive paradigm shift his personal life and then his congregation went through as he came to embrace relational leadership.

> The biblical role for the pastor begins by understanding that he is only one of the gift ministry people. Together they are to equip the saints to do the work of the ministry. The primary function of leadership is to equip and to train others in ministry functions. When the flock progresses beyond 25 people, one person cannot do it all.
>
> How therefore does a pastor spend his time? Primarily in the raising up of leaders![14]

The briefest survey of Scripture shows that team ministry has always been the model. Jesus had the one, John; then Peter and James; then the Twelve. James had the Apostolic Council at Jerusalem. Paul had his team of Timothy, Silas, Luke and others.

Many make the mistake that team ministry and leadership mean that there is no one leader. They go for an ideal of plurality in leadership where unanimous decisions are necessary for forward progress. I do not believe that is what Scripture is calling for. Larry Kreider shares how he and his team learned some of these lessons the hard way.

> We had encouraged the believers in the first house fellowship to designate no one person as leader, but instead to choose a team that would provide coequal leadership. The church was led by six coequal leaders. On the surface this sounded good and noble; in reality it was a manifestation of false humility. Underneath the surface, there was a struggle.
>
> Within the first year, this "leaderless group" came to realize that there was the need for clear, delegated leadership among us. Although we continued to believe that team leadership was important, we recognized the need for "headship" on each team.[15]

BUT I'M NOT A LEADER

If you are not in a "position" of leadership, perhaps you have been reading the past few pages, agreeing in theory with what is being said, but feeling that it applies more to pastors and ministry leaders than to you. I would like to challenge you!

First of all, relational Christianity is about you, the individual. Before we have relational leadership, we must have relational Christianity. That begins with each of us as individuals.

Recall for a moment the indicators of authentic relationship. Do you have a few, key individuals with whom you are committed to developing intentional relationships? Are you actively opening your life to the voice of the Lord through the "iron sharpening iron" of relationships? Whether your local church is intentional about relationship through small groups or not, you can actively begin to cultivate these relationships in your life that will nurture you to strength and health. You can begin to give and receive encouragement as you pursue your destiny in God. You can come to the place of authority in God where one puts a thousand to flight, but two put ten thousand. (See Deuteronomy 32:30.)

Do you want that kind of spiritual authority in your life? Are you ready to become dangerous to the kingdom of darkness? Then be honest with yourself in this moment. Decide to break through walls of self-protection and superficiality and come to the place of true relationship through walking out the indicators mentioned earlier. Come into a place of power and freedom by yoking yourself to relationship in the body.

ENEMIES TO OVERCOME

Don't be fooled! This is no small thing we are talking about! All of hell rages against the body coming into the health of unity. Multitudes of demonic assignments center around stirring up strife, creating accusation and generating offense. The level of spiritual warfare designed to prevent authentic Christian unity is vast.

How did Jesus say the world would know we were His disciples? Was it through our ministries? Through supernatural signs? Through influence on secular governments? Through our worship? Through ministry to the poor?

No. All of these things are right and necessary. But Jesus said the world would know we were His disciples, not by our outward activity, but *rather by the quality of life evidenced in the community of the redeemed.*

"These things I command you, that you love one another" (John 15:17, NKJV). Love one another—not tolerate, put up with, agree to disagree or cooperate. He said, "Love one another." How? "This is My commandment, that you love one another as I have loved you" (John 15:12, NKJV). In other words, with the same quality of love I have shown to you, the same openness, the same honesty, the same intimacy, the same vulnerability, the same selflessness, with *this* type of love, you are to love one another. "By this all will know that you are My disciples, if you have love for one another" (John 13:35, NKJV). This, then, is to be the ultimate apologetic of the church to the world—the ultimate proof that God is truly in our midst. The healings, the preaching, the social outreach, the worship is wonderful! But the thing that will prove to the world that Emmanuel is with us is the evidence of the quality of love and life we walk with one another! *True love, the kind that lays its life down for its friend, is the one thing the enemy cannot counterfeit.* Other aspects of our Christian experience can be done with human or demonic power, but only the love of God can produce the kind of love that results in loving, living Christian community.

Here are some of the strongholds that will war against this, both at the personal and the ministry leadership level.

- Pride
- Fear of intimacy
- Insecurity
- Need to control through manipulation
- Fear of personal cost
- Shame
- Apathy, or satisfaction with the status quo

- Fear of loss of position or influence
- Fear of being hurt
- Deception ("It's not so bad.")
- Comparison ("I/We are doing much better than him/them.")
- Fear of financial repercussions

Much could be said about each of these and many more. These are demonic strongholds that manifest as systems of thought in individuals and corporate bodies. They must be fully attacked through prayer, intercession and worship. There is also another strategy for battle here! We must combat these strongholds by coming against them with the opposite spirit. For example, if you are discerning that your church or relational group is battling a stronghold of shame, you may need to be bold and humble yourself, confessing something that you have battled with, in order to welcome in the spirit of the Father to combat that shame. If you sense a spirit of control operating in your church or group, then look for any area you may be manipulative or controlling (however pure and righteous your motive seems) and repent. Repentance, honesty and responding in the opposite spirit set in motion a divine chain reaction, a domino effect, that allows the Holy Spirit to move.

The world is a desert wasteland, void of the water of relationship. The modern American church has, by and large, been a mirage that has created hope but yielded disappointment. May we, by God's grace, dig deeply into the bedrock of His love, until the water of community gushes forth and releases streams in the desert.

What Now?

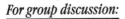

For group discussion:

1. We live in a very active and fast-paced society. Talk about how this affects your relationship with others, especially noting how difficult it is to cultivate time for quality relationships.

2. What changes could be made in the culture of your church that would facilitate relational development?

3. Look back at the section of this chapter that goes through the nine characteristics for authentic relationships. Spend an entire session discussing these characteristics with the purpose of establishing that authenticity in your group.

For personal application:

1. List three things that hinder you from growing in personal relationships.

2. Look back at the section on authentic relationships. Take note of characteristics or areas where you desire breakthrough and progress.

3. Consider the word *forgiveness*. Who is the first person who comes to your mind when you consider that word? Have you forgiven them? Are you seeking a restored relationship with them?

5

Creativity Unleashed

*The next generation will be fully
released in the power of creativity.*

Creativity is not just about the art, but the message behind it. Movies, television, music, magazines, computer screens and billboards all scream at us, vying for our attention and our dollars. But more often than not, what is being sold is not just a product, but a message. I am not talking about the old "if you use this deodorant/toothpaste/chewing gum you will look like this professional model and get this boyfriend/girlfriend" thing. We are all pretty wise to that. I am talking about a much deeper communication of values, philosophy and lifestyle that is bombarding us everywhere we go, consciously and subconsciously.

Philosophies—mind-sets—with roots in powerful, dark spiritual forces warring for the souls of this generation are being communicated through advertisements for mundane products like jeans and sneakers. The prince of darkness is bloodthirsty for the souls of this generation. All the while we are largely blind to the spiritual messages being sent out through the hundreds, and perhaps thousands, of images that invade our senses every day. Flying on the wings of creativity, impulses of licentiousness and rebellious independence are shot like arrows into our consciousness, and we don't even realize it. We think we have seen a commercial for sneakers; in reality we have experienced a message of individualism and humanistic reliance on self. We think we have seen an ad for clothing; in reality we have experienced an invitation to a lifestyle of soulish power and sexual "freedom."

Though we may not act on these impulses, it is impossible to measure their impact on our souls and more urgently, on the souls of our children. Innocence wanes, fantasies tempt and our eyes are clouded by a haze of seductive evil masquerading as the "lifestyle of the nineties." Values are conveyed through subtle messages that creatively captivate our imaginations. All of this is accomplished through the tool, the vehicle, of creativity.

Well, guess what? God, our God, is the source and wellspring of all creativity! And this generation is about to take back, with a vengeance, the tools of communication that have been handed over to the dark side.

You may have heard it taught that the church will recapture the arts. I believe we will not simply recapture the arts, but we will receive the spirit of creativity, the motivating power behind the arts. Artistic expression will be restored for use in worship, and we will also have released upon us the spirit of creativity—the ability to create new and more powerful songs and sounds, dances and dramas, pictures and sculptures. I believe the church will even soar into new art forms as vehicles of worship and evangelism.

THE TEMPLE AND THE MARKETPLACE

Two of the primary locations for the ministry of the early church were the temple and the marketplace. The arena of creativity captures the essence of both of the arenas in our society today. As fewer and fewer people attend a church or any religious meeting with any regularity, they attempt to meet the needs of their soul through artistic experiences. Concerts from artists like Yanni, John Tesh and the Three Tenors have become the new temple; Riverdance, Stomp and Cirque de Soleil, the new marketplaces.

Social scientist John Naisbitt, in his book *Megatrends 2000*, documents the rise of the importance of creativity and the arts in our culture today.

[This decade] will bring forth a modern renaissance in the visual arts, poetry, dance and theater throughout the developed world. New York's Broadway Theater at Broadway and Fifty-third sells more tickets than either the Giants or the Jets. Professional dance has grown 700% in the past 20 years in America. Opera audiences have tripled in the past two decades.[1]

There is ample evidence that the world is flocking to the arts as never before as an answer for their search for meaning. The arts are no longer just about the medium, but now they too are all about the message. Tens of thousands recently gathered at the Washington Mall for the Tibetan Freedom Concert. The rock stars of this generation gathered with Buddhist monks in orange robes to protest the injustice of the Chinese and show support for the plight of the Tibetans. And, of course, they opened themselves up to be influenced by the Buddhist message.

SOLI DEO GLORIA

I won't belabor the point that has been made so many times, but it is clear from church history that the church once set the standard for artistic expression throughout the world. From Michelangelo's Sistine Chapel to J. S. Bach's oratorios to Handel's *Messiah,* the church set the standard for beauty and excellence. Art was a discipline that ultimately produced works dedicated to God. Whether the artists themselves actually had a personal walk with God varies, of course, and with some we will never know. But the fact remained that the church saw as part of its mission the responsibility of telling the story of the Lord by introducing expressions of excellence and beauty to the world.

But we can look back much farther than the church. The Old Testament gives many accounts of anointing resting on artists and their work and describes their talent being consecrated to the Lord.

In Exodus 31 the anointing of the Lord rested on those who were to fashion the house of God. Their abilities were seen not just as natural talent, but as a supernatural endowment for kingdom purposes.

Then the LORD said to Moses, "See, I have chosen Bezalel son of Uri, the son of Hur, of the tribe of Judah, *and I have filled him with the Spirit of God, with skill, ability and knowledge in all kinds of crafts*—to make artistic designs for work in gold, silver and bronze, to cut and set stones, to work in wood, and to engage in all kinds of craftsmanship. Moreover, I have appointed Oholiab son of Ahisamach, of the tribe of Dan, to help him. Also I have given skill to all the craftsmen to make everything I have commanded you.

—EXODUS 31:1–6, EMPHASIS ADDED

It was not only visual beauty and excellence that surrounded the temple of the Lord. One cannot read the Old Testament without the clear understanding that God likes music! Imagine the cacophony of sound that accompanied the bringing up of the ark of the covenant into Jerusalem.

The musicians Heman, Asaph and Ethan were to *sound the bronze cymbals*; Zechariah, Aziel, Shemiramoth, Jehiel, Unni, Eliab, Maaseiah and Benaiah were to *play the lyres* according to alamoth, and Mattithiah, Eliphelehu, Mikneiah, Obed-Edom, Jeiel and Azaziah were to *play the harps,* directing according to sheminith. *Kenaniah the head Levite was in charge of the singing*; that was his responsibility because *he was skillful at it.*

Berekiah and Elkanah were to be doorkeepers for the ark. Shebaniah, Joshaphat, Nethanel, Amasai, Zechariah, Benaiah and Eliezer *the priests were to blow trumpets before the ark of God.* Obed-Edom and Jehiah were also to be doorkeepers for the ark.

So David and the elders of Israel and the commanders of units of a thousand went to bring up the ark of the covenant of the LORD from the house of Obed-Edom, with rejoicing. Because God had helped the Levites who were carrying the ark of the covenant of the LORD, seven bulls and seven rams were sacrificed. Now David was clothed in a robe of fine linen, as were all the Levites who were carrying the ark, *and as were the singers,* and Kenaniah, who was in charge of the *singing of the choirs.* David also wore a linen ephod.

So all Israel brought up the ark of the covenant of the LORD with shouts, with the sounding of rams' horns and trumpets, and of cymbals, and the playing of lyres and harps.

—1 CHRONICLES 15:19–28, EMPHASIS ADDED

It is clear then, from Scripture and church history, that artistic and creative expressions were not merely an appendage to worship, or something outside the realm occupied by God's people. Rather, those who were anointed by God in these giftings were to be recognized and released into their callings, believing that the creative spirit, which came from God, would bring glory to Him and in so doing, draw people's attention to God.

BE RELEASED

This generation will rise up with new anointing and authority in the creative domain; it will bring forth anointed sounds and sights that will glorify God and draw men to Jesus. Casting off the restraints of the spirit of religion, a torrent of creative power will break through the dam of fear and brittle dryness. The marrow of creative anointing will be released into the dry bones of dead religious institutions, bringing forth life.

In the past, rather than discipling, equipping and releasing our filmmakers, dancers, musicians and artists, we created a subculture called Christian art. We forced these talented believers to squeeze into that subculture rather than allow them to be salt and light to the kingdoms of this world. We did the exact opposite of what Jesus commanded when He said, "Go ye into all the world…" (Mark 16:15, KJV). He was not excluding the domain of creativity from the Great Commission. He is the Source of it and Lord of all! We are to go and raise a standard of righteous excellence in these realms and capture them for Him. We are not to hide the "light" of evangelistic creativity under the "bushel" of Christian subculture.

The limits we have placed on the spirit of creativity have been based in fear and the pride of our own ethnocentricity. Just as Saul's daughter Michal cursed David, our own barrenness of spirit has motivated our attack on those with the spirit of David. (See 2 Samuel 6:12–23.) All too often we label as fleshly, soulish or even demonic things that are simply outside the realm of our experience.

I will never forget taking our youth group to a regional worship event when I was a youth pastor in my first ministry position. A coalition of several youth groups sponsored these events from time to time, and I was on the steering committee. Most of the churches there were more mainline denominations, but my church had a more charismatic background. Our little youth group was anything but inhibited.

The worship team got going and began singing a song that said, "I will sing/dance/clap as David did." The other youth groups kind of stood there, halfheartedly mouthing the words. Our group viewed the words as an invitation to action and began to do exactly what the songs were calling for—clapping, shouting and (gasp!) dancing.

(For the life of me I have never understood why people sing songs and then refuse, don't allow or squelch the very thing the song is calling for!)

One of the other leaders came over to me, obviously very displeased and very flustered. "Don't you see what is happening?" he said. "These kids are dancing in the church!"

"No," the words came to me, "the church is dancing in the building."

Let the dancers dance! Let the singers sing! Let the writers write! Let the artisans create! All who were born for this hour to show forth the beauty of the Lord, to adorn His bride with garments of praise and to raise up His fallen tabernacle—hear the word of the Lord! Be free! Be released! Run to Him, and in His presence let the yearning of your heart to express your love and adoration for Him be restrained no more. It matters not if you are alone in your living room or in a congregation of thousands—yours is an audience of One. You sing, act, play, create, express for His pleasure and His pleasure alone.

EVANGELISM

There is an amazing strategy the Lord is using to bring in the harvest of souls in this hour. The singers and dancers will once again lead the army of God into the battlefield! Warring for the souls of a generation, these anointed creators will release the sounds and sights of heaven onto earth, and unbelievers will flock to them, sensing deep within their hearts that this is what they have been searching for all along. This is different from the crossover artists we have seen in the past. The new minstrels and artists will build a bridge, but the crossing over will be done by the world, by unbelievers streaming into the kingdom.

There are even now examples of this phenomenon. Martin Smith and Delirious, a Generation X worship band from England, have stayed true to their anointing, calling and message, yet they have gained amazing popularity with the general public.

In the realm of dance, Arts Triumphant Conservatory in Jacksonville, Florida, is on the prophetic cutting edge. Under the direction of Colin and Yvonne Williams, it is vitally networked into their local arts community and is seen as a viable and valuable addition to Jacksonville culture. Yvonne has had a successful career in the secular dance world, and so she is respected by her peers. Beyond that, Arts Triumphant is intentional about bringing its message to the world. Performances are often in neutral sites, such as local university campuses, which give dancers an opportunity to naturally and gracefully bring the Spirit of God with them into every venue they fill.

Yvonne and I were once invited to perform for the prime minister of Israel, Benjamin Netanyahu. As I sang and she danced at a semiprivate ceremony at his office, I was awed at how the Lord can use the gift of artistic expression to give us an opportunity to be His light.

At the conclusion of our performance, the prime minister commented on how he needs to be as flexible in dealing with the tense Middle East political situation as Yvonne is in her dance, and how he needs the help of God to do that. That very day he left for the Middle East peace talks at Wye Mills, Maryland. An October 1998 summit at Wye Mills, Maryland, generated the first real progress in the stymied Middle East peace talks in nineteen months. With President Clinton mediating—and a late assist from an ailing King Hussein of Jordan—Israeli Prime Minister Benjamin Netanyahu and Palestinian President Yasir Arafat settled several important interim issues called for by the 1993 Oslo Peace Accords.[2]

Another example of the spirit of creativity being released and setting a new standard which then gives way to evangelism is Veggie Tales. These are animated children's programs that even the adults on our staff love to watch!

While pioneering powerful new technology in computer animation, the antics of Larry the Cucumber and Bob the Tomato are hysterical, but they also deliver biblical and moral lessons without compromise. The popularity of these shows has already expanded outside the church. I expect to see a real rise in their success in the secular world as the world realizes there is an alternative to the insanity and darkness of most Saturday cartoons.

CROSS-CULTURAL MUSIC EVANGELISM

Overseas, and in cross-cultural settings, the use of indigenous sight and sound goes a long way toward letting people know Jesus is not a white, middle-aged American in a Brooks Brothers suit. He is not an American Jesus but the Lord of the nations who became flesh and whose Spirit is incarnational. Following is an insightful discussion of this reality, as reported by Frank Fortunato of the AD 2000 organization. It begins with a testimony of an Indian Christian who heard Indian-style worship music for the first time.

"When I first heard the sitar being used to worship Jesus Christ, my hair stood on end and my hands tingled. It was drawing out the worship in me. It was like my natural inbred feelings were being released by hearing sounds we have been brought up to relate to. Through this music both parts of our blended culture are being reached."

These were early discoveries made by Asian Ram Gidoomal in learning to relate his Indian background and music to his new home situation in the UK. As the world's cities continue to become melting pots of cultures, Ram and many other believers like him grapple with the way they should worship in such culturally mixed settings.

This led Ram to form South Asia Concern (SAC), an outreach ministry based in Surrey, UK. The ministry uses the arts and unique evangelistic approaches to reach the Asian youth as well as disciple Asian believers in the UK. One product that emerged from SAC has become a classic among Britain's Asian community. It's a CD called

Asia Worships, and it blends East and West like few Christian recordings to date.

Tony Cummings, a well-known British music communicator captured his first reactions to the *Asia Worships* recording: "Tablas fuse with Flemish bagpipes and synths swirl around sitars in unforgettable landscapes. In an age where the electronic realities of the global village mean that the West is coming alive to different cultures and musics like no other one and where God's Spirit is thrillingly beginning to breathe over a whole continent for so long cloaked in spiritual darkness, here is an album to reflect these truths."

Ram picks up the story: "The album was conceived as a means of giving Asian Christians in Britain a culturally relevant worship resource. I found that many young Asian Christians were becoming disillusioned and leaving the Church because they felt completely isolated, no longer Hindu but still Asian, not English or Western. The tracks that resulted featured a blend of British, American, Indian and Pakistani musicians. We then went to London's Kensington Temple (a church with more than 50 nationalities represented) where a choir of Asian Christians from charismatic to orthodox churches came together." The recording has crossed the oceans and is being played globally.

Another aspect of cultural adjustments takes place when believers want to inject new meaning into existing art forms that have traditionally had a non-Christian use. A recent article was devoted to these issues. One article explained that when a Christian church in Singapore planned to present a "redeemed" Chinese lion dance, some of the believers were understandably perturbed. They wondered how this could be right. They knew that the traditional Chinese meanings of the lion dance were certainly not Christ-centered.

Wisely, the artists who had adapted the ancient Chinese dance presented an extensive time of teaching before the performance, explaining the new Christian meanings. The dance went on and it was well received by the believers and understood by non-Christians as well.

Commenting on this story, Randy and Nicole McCaskill, missionaries in Bali, point out that the experience in Singapore illustrates clearly the need to teach the Christian meaning for the art form when using traditional, culturally loaded artistic expressions and forms.

The article then moved to Bali where yet another issue was discussed of the issues involved in adapting cultural forms to worship. One Balinese church presented the complete "Srigati harvest dance" without changing any of the traditional choreography. However, they did apply a completely new Christian meaning to each part of the dance. The church took definite steps to help its congregation truly understand what it was seeing. An illustrator was engaged to sketch the dance's six major thematic moves. The artists then added a descriptive portion of Scripture to each drawing. Next, the church compiled the illustrations and Scriptures into a pamphlet that was given to the audience. Before each performance, a pastor reinforced the new messages of the dance for the Balinese audience.

One believer created a dance to symbolize the Holy Spirit. It was very innovative, yet kept to Balinese-style movements. The dance actually contributed to the development of Balinese dance in Bali, at the same time communicating a new, Christ-centered message to Balinese culture. Balinese Christian artists are on the cutting edge of creativity, according to the McCaskills. They can be perceived as contributors to and redeemers of culture rather than as destroyers, which is the most common accusation hurled at Christians by anthropologists.[3]

These are excellent examples of what happens when we allow Jesus to be Jesus, not our culturally limited picture of Him. He makes Himself known within cultural expressions and frees believers to worship Him in the styles innate to them. He reaches out to the unbelievers of that culture through sound and sight experiences that are relevant to them. His voice is heard.

GET OUT THOSE PAINT BRUSHES

You may be an artist who is bursting with creativity just waiting to be released, or you may be a believer gifted in other areas who is waiting to be blessed by what is brought forth through these modern-day Bezalels and Kenaniahs. Either way, here are some practical steps you can take to open up your life and church to the creative spirit.

Consecrate your gift to the Lord.

Our identity can never be rooted in our abilities or talents. These must not become idols that keep us from Him. Lay your gifts down regularly before Him, forfeiting your right to them and inviting His cleansing and anointing. Pride must be resisted.

I will never forget being in Israel a few years ago. I was the assistant producer for an international conference sponsored by Dr. David Yonggi Cho, the pastor of the world's largest church, which is located in Seoul, Korea.

I had been working with the worship team on this one particular piece, the grand finale. It had all kinds of dance, banners and incredible music. We were scheduled to close the entire conference with this piece, which included a processional of the flags of all the nations. We poured ourselves into this piece, rehearsing long hours and really praying, sensing an anointing on it as it declared the lordship of Messiah over all the nations of the world.

Finally, the last session of the conference came. There were several speakers in the final session, and many of them went considerably over their scheduled time. Finally Dr. Cho's assistant came backstage to let me know that the meeting had gone too late. It was almost 11:00 P.M.; when this speaker finished, Dr. Cho was going to dismiss the conference in prayer. The grand finale had been canceled.

Instantly I was faced with a choice—anger and frustration, or trust. I would feel either used and unappreciated, or content in God. I breathed a prayer and received such grace from the Lord. In the background I heard Dr. Cho dismiss the conference.

Quickly I gathered the worship team and dancers and told them to get ready to go on. "Why?" they asked. "The hall is virtually empty. Everyone is leaving. There is no one to hear us."

"Yes, there is," I replied.

We got the sound man to roll the tape, and in the huge, empty hall in the International Convention Center in Jerusalem we began singing and dancing and declaring that Messiah is Lord over all the nations of the earth. As I sang, I was flushed with a sense of the pleasure of the Lord and what He was accomplishing through us at that moment. A few moments earlier we had been focused on declaring these truths to several thousand people. Now our focus was on another realm. We were strongly declaring before the grandstands of heaven and the grandstands of hell, before angels and demons, before the "great cloud of witnesses" and before the Lord Himself, the truth of His Word (Heb. 12:1).

As performers our attitude must always be one of offering up *to the Lord* all we do, content for Him to use us in whatever ways He sees fit, visible or not. Today, several years after this experience, I still feel strongly that we were prophesying that night into unseen arenas, sowing seeds of worship and warfare into heavenly realms with results that are very real, though immeasurable.

Educate yourself in the arts.

Maybe you have never been to a symphony or seen Shakespeare or been to your local art museum. Find out what is going on in your community. This is where the lost are! This does not have to be costly; many museums and shows are free or very inexpensive. Take your home group or prayer partner and go to a museum one day, and bring Jesus with you. Discuss the art you see in relationship to your Christianity. Ask the Lord for divine appointments and opportunities to witness.

Encourage creativity.

In your local church, look for opportunities to push the creative envelope past the usual Sunday morning hymn. The Scripture reading could be acted out in drama. Instead of a soloist offering a special song one morning, what about a painter offering a special picture, or a mime offering a piece? In one of our Eagles' Wings conferences recently, we invited a twenty-year-old art student who is a believer to paint on the platform while the worship team worshiped. At the end of the worship time, she shared her painting with the congregation along with the impressions she had received from the Lord. It was a quickly done painting and might not win any awards, but it allowed us to see there is a place for her gift in the church. God-given creativity will make a place for many gifts that have not been used in the church in the past!

Develop your own gifts.

So many times people have played musical instruments or had creative pursuits but have laid them down for one reason or another. Pick them back up! You may never be great in man's eyes in your gift, but you are not offering it to man, but to the Lord. Allow your gift to be a place where your intercession can come forth—a new way of pouring your heart out to the Lord.

Develop the gifts of others.

What if local churches got together in cities and towns and organized performing arts schools? So many public schools are cutting back on music programs that there is a great need for this. These after-school and Saturday classes could be staffed by believers and offer quality training with Christian-based musical curriculum. It could be a wonderful bridge to develop relationships with unbelievers and, if run properly, could pay for itself and even produce a profit. Or, another idea in this regard is to be a patron to a young artist. Find a young person in your church who wants to learn trumpet or dance or sculpture. Agree to help pay for his or her lessons as long as this student remains serious about developing his or her gift. Pour some finances and encouragement into the heart of one of tomorrow's leaders.

Whatever the Lord speaks to you, do it with all your might. The world is flocking right now to the temple of the arts, but the Lord is raising up a living temple of creators following *the* Creator. This generation will release the sounds of heaven, which will melt men's hearts and cause a generation to come to know the greatest Artist of all, the One who has painted our destiny in crimson.

What Now?

For group discussion:

1. Make a list of which creative arts are used in your church. Then make a list of arts that aren't, and discuss why they are not.

2. In what ways has your church's culture impacted the type of creative expression released in its services?

3. Discuss the ways that the arts impact culture. Is it important that Christians are involved in the arts? Why or why not?

For personal application:

1. What are the creative expressions—such as singing, writing, wood-work—that you enjoy? Don't consider whether you excel at them or not; simply consider the ones you enjoy.

2. Consider a talent that you used to use but do not any longer. Why don't you pursue it any more? Would you like to? What would you have to do to grow in this ability again?

3. Zephaniah says that God sings. It seems that He paints the sky every night. Do a Scripture study considering the creativity of God.

One Body,
Diverse Members

*The next generation will be intentional in reconciliation.
It will embrace the strengths found in other cultures
and seek to honor others and learn from them.*

For the past several years, Eagles' Wings has organized short-term missions teams from the United States to work with several local fellowships throughout Honduras. Pastors Luis and Pam Perez, associate ministers from Bethel Full Gospel Church in Rochester, New York, provide leadership. On the last few days of our trip we sponsor a conference at a retreat center and have a few days of fellowship, discipleship and genuine relationship building with our Honduran brothers and sisters in Christ.

In the midst of worship at one of these conferences a few years ago, the Lord began dealing with my heart. I was deeply convicted that much of what the American church had exported was more involved with American mind-sets than it was with the pure gospel. I pondered so much of what I had seen throughout Honduras and Central America over the past years of ministry. So many problems—division, competition and a performance mentality—were the result of many Central American leaders copying what had been modeled for them in North America. I was not under false guilt—I recognized much good that the American church had done—but I felt deep conviction from the Holy Spirit.

In the midst of worship I shared this with Pastor Perez, and I asked the Central American pastors who were there to join us on the stage. I repented before them for the poor example America had set in so many areas, asked their forgiveness and asked the Lord to break off of them any false mind-sets or systems that our example had brought. As this unfolded, there was an amazing change in the atmosphere. You could sense the Holy Spirit descending and blessing what was taking place.

A group of Koreans happened to be in the service that night. I asked them to come up on the platform and join us as we corporately entered back into worship. We began to sing out spontaneously. First the Hondurans sang in Spanish, then the Koreans in Korean, followed by the Americans in English. Then everyone sang together in their native tongue.

The breakthrough that took place in that service was incredible. Remembering it now, even a few years later, my eyes fill with tears at the special presence of the Lord that was manifested that night. We had a taste of the tremendous diversity and blessing God has given us in the nations and people groups of the world.

WHAT THE WORLD NEEDS NOW

There was a song in the seventies that said love is what the world needs now. This is definitely true! We have only to look at the global tensions to see how desperate we are for peace. Israel and the Palestinians; Northern Ireland; racial tension in South Africa; Hindus vs. Moslems in India; racial strife throughout America. It seems that the more we talk about multiculturalism and acceptance, the less tolerance we have toward one another.

In the midst of this cultural war zone, Jesus has called believers to be the peacemakers. He has called us to become a force for justice and peace in the midst of troubled times.

Blessed are the peacemakers, for they will be called sons of God.
—MATTHEW 5:9

If you study this word *peacemaker* in the Greek, it carries the idea of action behind it. In other words, it is not saying blessed are those who simply keep to themselves and hope everyone else does the same. To the contrary, the idea expressed here is that we will be called the sons of God if we actively seek to bring about peace in situations where there is strife and division. This verse carries with it the call to intentionality.

The classic *Adam Clarke Commentary* describes the activity required of peacemakers.

> A peace-maker is a man who, being endowed with a generous public spirit, labours for the public good, and feels his own interest promoted in promoting that of others: therefore, instead of fanning the fire of strife, he uses his influence and wisdom to reconcile the contending parties, adjust their differences, and restore them to a state of unity. As all men are represented to be in a state of hostility to God and each other, the Gospel is called the Gospel of peace, because it tends to reconcile men to God and to each other.[1]

Throughout the body of Christ we are being called to reconciliation. Dividing walls are being broken down—Jew and Gentile, black and white, Hispanic and Asian, old and young, male and female, rich and poor. The body is beginning to understand how desperately all parts are needed. We cannot be complete until each portion and each member of the body is released into the fullness of their divine purpose. How may we hasten this process? How do we become peacemakers?

REPENTANCE

We must recognize the call of the Scripture to *intentionality*. In other words, anything less than actively seeking the kingdom is falling short. Neutrality is not acceptable. If we are not part of the solution, then we are part of the problem. And we need to repent.

Personal repentance is honestly acknowledging whatever strongholds, or "houses of thought" (thought patterns), we have harbored. (See chapter 7 for more teaching on strongholds.) Have we secretly thought less of those from a culture different from our own? Have we thought them lazy? Elitist? Irresponsible? Self-centered? Do we harbor fear about those who are different from ourselves? Have we entertained stereotypes and generalizations and reinforced them to our families and friends?

Have we actively sought out those different from us—white, black, Asian, Hispanic, Jew, rich, poor, less educated, more educated? Have we reached out with a hand of friendship, offering acceptance and relationship? If we are simply content to declare our innocence —"I am not a racist!"—but put no action to our words, then our statements, without works, are dead.

The church as a whole has not taken action, as George Barna points out:

> The Caucasian population is at zero population growth, while the African American, Hispanic and Asian populations in our country are experiencing double digit expansion. By 2050, only half of America's population will be Caucasian. Ethnic diversity is here to stay, and racial reconciliation is a national concern, *but the church remains our most segregated institution.*[2]

Most churches in America today would loudly trumpet their innocence, declaring that they are very open to people of other backgrounds attending their services. But drastic times call for drastic measures. The fabric of our society is unraveling. No longer can we allow passivity to be the rule of the day. The time is now for drastic, intentional communication and commitment to relational healing before it is too late and our cities—and suburbs—go up in flames.

Ask yourself these questions: Am I actively pursuing relationship with anyone whose background is very different from my own? Am I seeking to understand them—their background, their frame of reference? Am I providing opportunities for real dialogue to occur? If not, commit to it now. Commit to growing in relationship with someone from a background very different from your own.

At a group level, God has been leading people to take action through identificational repentance. Identificational repentance is standing in representation of others—your race, church, ancestors, gender—and before the Lord and one another asking forgiveness and pledging behavior leading to healing.

John Dawson, in his landmark bestseller *Healing America's Wounds,* lays a foundation for identificational repentance.

> We can all identify with the roots of any given sin. Take, for example...abortion. You may never have participated in an abortion, but all of us have been guilty of the root sins that give place to such an activity. I can think of five common roots that lead to abortion: lust, the love of comfort, the love of money, rejection and unbelief. These are struggles common to all and illustrate, therefore, the need for honest identification with the sins of our nation when we "stand in the gap" (Ezek. 22:30) asking for God's mercy for our nation.
>
> Nehemiah and the families with him assembled themselves before the Lord with fasting, in sackcloth, and with dust on their heads. Though they were just a remnant, they completely identified with their nation and its history. "Then those of Israelite lineage separated themselves from the foreigners; and they stood and confessed their sins and the iniquities of their fathers" (Neh. 9:2, [NKJV]).
>
> As we stand in the gap for America, we allow the Holy Spirit to shine the bright light of truth into the inner rooms of our souls. We run from the religious deceit that would seduce us into believing that we are superior to any person.[3]

This generation is kneeling down in humble penitence, asking the Father to "forgive our sin and heal our land." Far from the heart of the self-righteous Pharisee who thanked God that he was not like other sinners, there is a cry rising up deep in our souls that says we are indeed sinners and that we who are of the household of faith are all the more responsible because of the great measure of grace that has been poured out upon us.

INTERCESSION

True repentance, both personal and identificational, will deposit within us a burden to pray for those from whom we previously distanced ourselves or maligned. Compassion will well up in our souls as we genuinely ask the Lord to bring grace, mercy and healing to peoples and cultures with whom we were formerly unacquainted.

A few years ago at an Eagles' Wings conference I was made aware that one of the chiefs of the Apache nation from an Arizona reservation was in attendance. I had the privilege of meeting him, and, in one of our evening sessions, I introduced him to the conference attendees and invited him to share a greeting.

As he spoke, the Holy Spirit prompted a time of repentance and reconciliation. Several leaders stood in identificational repentance and moved into a time of blessing the Native American people, especially the Apache nation this brother represented. We then learned that immediately following the conference this man and his wife were leaving for their first trip to Israel to celebrate the Feast of Tabernacles. We began to bless him on his pilgrimage to Israel and then felt led to pray for the peace of Jerusalem. I prayed in English, followed by the chief, who prayed in Apache. At this point, the Messianic Jews who were present came forward weeping, deeply touched at hearing a prayer for Jerusalem in Apache!

This led to a general call for reconciliation. African American and Hispanic pastors came and joined the Apache brother, the Messianic leaders and the Anglos. What a sight! A deep release of weeping and healing swept throughout the congregation, followed by a joyful time of worship and praise as we all sensed that this unity was a bit of what God has in store for His body!

Since this experience my heart has developed a deeper sensitivity and compassion for Native American people. Was I prejudiced against them before? Certainly not consciously. But neither was I actively, intentionally seeking to bless and see them reconciled to God and society. But when I put a face and a name to my head knowledge about Native Americans, something in my spirit was activated and it has changed me. Our ministry actively prays for this Apache brother now, and we have been able to bless him in practical ways as well. We are working to become part of the solution, not bystanders muttering in frustration while the problem worsens.

Intercession almost always leads to relationship. It is difficult to stay distanced from people you are praying for and for whom the Lord is filling you with compassion. As the bonds of relationship and unity strengthen, each joint supplies what the other lacks, and the body moves toward greater health and authority.

Pastor Joseph Garlington, a leader of leaders, offers this mandate urging us toward reconciliation.

> I can live with the pain of racial rejection, gender rejection, or religious rejection, but the only way to truly overcome is to become a "minister of reconciliation." *The only true authorized medium of this message is the Church of Jesus.* If we don't do it, we will live with the consequences of our disobedience. The Church must rise above her identity in ethnicity and gender, above denominationalism and sectarianism, and get on with the business of making disciples of all the nations. It's going to take the whole Church to reach the whole world, and that world is cross-racial and cross-cultural. If we don't do it, the consequences are even more frightening than one would want to contemplate.[4]

To enter into intercession for a people group is to allow the Lord to fill your heart with a sensitivity to what they have suffered. Let's face it, the world is full of pain and injustice, and no one escapes it at some level. To have empathy with a group is not to take up its offense. Offense and bitterness will only bear poisonous fruit. But empathy will allow you to hear the other side and to absorb the reality of their situation. The only way to move toward truth is to place yourself in another's situation because perception is often the people's reality. This is true for individuals as well as for entire people groups.

God the Father, the ultimate reconciler, did this for us. Our cause was certainly not "just." We were sinners, alienated from God by our own sin and depravity. But if we were to be reached, a bridge had to be created. So God put himself "in our shoes!" Emmanuel—God with us!

> For we do not have a high priest who is unable to sympathize with our weaknesses, but we have one who has been tempted in every way, just as we are—yet was without sin.
>
> —HEBREWS 4:15

The reason we have been able to find God and be reconciled to Him is because He made Himself accessible and tangible to us in the person of His Son. This is the ultimate model of reconciliation. We must become willing to understand the pain of another and take them by the hand. Together, let's walk toward the health of a tomorrow not based on the past, with its blaming and self-pity, but toward a future of a hope—based on forgiveness.

One great example I know of a person living out this principle is my dear friend Reuven Doron. Reuven is a native Israeli, born in Tel Aviv. He is a believer in Yeshua (Jesus) and a leading voice in the Messianic movement around the world. As an Israeli, he holds strong feelings of nationalism and supports the State of Israel. He also has clear and strong views on the "land for peace" policies of Yasir Arafat and the PLO.

Nevertheless, Reuven made it his business to care for the Arabs in the Gaza Strip, where approximately one million Palestinians live in squalid conditions. Reuven has teamed up with a missionary living there and is regularly sponsoring young Palestinian children with heart conditions and other treatable, life-threatening problems—bringing them to Israel for surgery and medical care. Imagine! An Israeli, devoted to his people and country, who has the breadth of compassion to reach out with the love of God to those this world would call his enemies.

"I am an Israeli," says Reuven, "but first I am a believer. My love for Yeshua mandates that I move toward helping those in need wherever and whoever they are. I am not released from the commandments of Yeshua 'unto the least of these' simply because of political strife. Before I am a citizen of Israel, I am a citizen of the kingdom."

This is intentional reconciliation—repenting for heart attitudes and then actively pursuing relationship and blessing with those from whom you were formerly alienated.

John Dawson lists fifteen potential areas for "conflict and broken relationship." See how many of these situations you can identify with.

- Race to race (i.e., Native American vs. European American)
- Class to class (i.e., homeless person vs. holders of home equity)
- Culture to culture (i.e., immigrant vs. native born)
- Gender to gender (i.e., working woman vs. male hierarchy)
- Vocation to vocation (i.e., L.A. Police Department vs. civil rights workers)
- Institution to institution (i.e., auto industry management vs. organized labor)
- Region to region (i.e., Westside vs. South Central Los Angeles)
- Governed to government (i.e., college-age youth vs. Vietnam-era government)
- Religion to religion (i.e., Muslim vs. Christian)
- Denomination to denomination (i.e., Protestant vs. Catholic)
- Enterprise to enterprise (i.e., monopoly vs. small business)
- Idealogy to idealogy (i.e., leftist vs. rightist political parties)
- Nationality to nationality (i.e., Americans vs. Cubans)
- Generation to generation (i.e., youth vs. parents)
- Family to family (i.e., neighbor vs. neighbor)[5]

How many of these classifications can you place yourself within? Are you being intentional about reconciling with those who are different from you? Are you breaking down stereotypes with those you influence, or are you reinforcing them?

I was raised in a Protestant, evangelical home, but all of my extended family was Catholic. I remember hearing reinforced over and over again from my parents and our churches how deceived and heretical "those Catholics" were. It was amazing how much time was spent tearing down this particular denomination! This was drilled into my way of thinking, so when I would go to our relatives homes and be with them I immediately felt alienated from them. I was so sorry for them, and a bit suspicious of them, thinking that it must be awful to be without God.

This stereotype carried over into my first years of ministry as an adult and broadened to include anyone from any mainline church. Surely none of the people in mainline churches were truly saved—only we evangelicals were!

This continued until I became part of a cross-denominational network of youth ministries that met monthly in our area. I met scores of youth leaders and youth from Lutheran, Presbyterian, Methodist, United Church of Christ and (gasp!) Catholic churches who had genuine relationships with Jesus Christ and were seeking to know Him more! I was angry at the conditioning I was given and ashamed of the judgmental attitude I had carried for far too long.

I understand the need for preaching a clear salvation message emphasizing a personal relationship with Christ, and I do wish and pray that mainline churches would emphasize this vital part of our faith more. In fact, there are many valiant believers who have felt directed of the Lord to fight for renewal and orthodoxy within these denominations. The point is not the practice or even doctrine of these churches (some of which may be heretical). The point is that I dismissed people, *brothers and sisters in Christ,* without giving them the benefit of even a conversation, simply because of a label. Worse yet, my life was influencing others toward the same smallness of spirit. May we come to the place where we treat people as individuals and remove the walls of stereotypes that keep us boxed in from one another.

We certainly cannot give a thorough overview to all the different classifications where we as the body should move as reconcilers. I would, however, like to highlight two that seem to be especially important at this time.

INTERGENERATIONAL RECONCILIATION

The world is free-falling, without moral or ethical structures to hold it in place. We are far more technologically advanced but becoming far less civilized as a people. Common courtesy, basic manners, a strong work ethic and essential moral fiber that were expected in the past are fading. The threads of decency that have woven the fabric of a safe and good society are unraveling.

We can lament these realities. We can ignore them. But, we do either of these at our peril. There is a third option. We can join the rising tide of realistic yet hopeful healers and work for change. This will require humility and great strength. But it is the only path to health.

Repentance

The older generations seem to express outrage and shame at the attitudes and conduct of "Generation X," without pausing to consider what their role has been in forming the personality of this generation. Consider these thoughts from William Bennett's book *The Index of Leading Cultural Indicators.*

> In contrast to the 3 hours per day they spend watching TV, teenagers spend an average of *5 minutes per day* alone with their fathers. A Carnegie Corporation report found that even the time teenagers spend with their families consists primarily of eating or watching television together.[6]
>
> The United States has the highest divorce rate in the world...approximately half of all U.S. marriages can be expected to end in divorce.[7]

Senator Daniel Patrick Moynihan has written:

> There is one unmistakable lesson in human history: A community that allows a large number of young men to grow up in broken families, dominated by women, never acquiring any rational expectations about the future—that community asks for and gets chaos. In such a society, crime, violence, unrest, unrestrained lashing out at the whole social structure—these are not only to be expected, they are nearly inevitable.[8]

The chaos we are facing as a people is a result of idolatry. Vainly, we have pursued money, status and this world's definition of success. We have tolerated a church system with an insane pressure to look right and act right, regardless of what unspoken needs lie beneath the surface. We have been too arrogant to admit our weaknesses. And our churches have not been climates where weakness can be readily admitted. We have not walked in covenant with God or one another. We have been in this world, and this world has been in us.

The first step toward reconciliation between the current generations will require repentance. The kind of change we need will require deep and life-changing repentance, not a superficial, emotional response. We need a repentance as deep as our wound, and our national, intergenerational wound is life-threatening.

This will cost us something. I know one large church that began to get serious about deeply examining their church life and culture and asking the Lord to reveal what was hollow, insincere and simply repetitive. The pastor called for eight weeks of repentance. The Sunday services became sober and focused, without a lot of solos, choir songs and upbeat praise. He felt the Lord was calling the body to a season of the deep dealings of the Lord, and that it needed to be for the whole body, not just the small percentage who might show up on Sunday or Wednesday night.

After only three weeks there was a great release of anger and frustration for a large percentage of the congregation. Many felt he had gone overboard. They had repented for two weeks now, what else was needed? Some of the people who had been with the church for years were furious and threatening.

Within six weeks, two hundred fifty people had left the church. Finally, around the ninth or tenth week, there was a breakthrough. A rebirth of divine presence and purpose filled the congregation. New leadership emerged. They were flooded with fresh strategies for inner health and growth and outward impact. Soon, church growth was experienced, not just from transfer growth, but from new converts coming to the Lord.

This generation bears deep scars of rejection, alienation and abuse. In order for us to move ahead, the elders must accept responsibility and repent. This is happening in some ways in the Promise Keepers movement, but it must become localized. We need the same type of exchange between generations that we have seen in public repentance and forgiveness between ethnic groups. There must be an intentional coming together of generations for healing to flow.

THE CHURCH AS PARENT

This is a parentless generation. The one parent that many children have left after a divorce is consumed with working and survival. Schools no longer provide a moral influence. The provision of even basic education or training in life skills is on the decline.

The church will begin to understand its role as a parenting influence—as a holistic life-growth community. The people of this generation need someone to teach them how to change the oil in their cars, how to garden, how to sew, how to vote, how to cook, how to manage money, how to raise their own children. Though strong in its understanding of technology, this generation is weak in basic life skills. Where will it go to learn these things? Families are not intact; schools and government have failed.

Into this void, the church of Jesus Christ must come. We cannot truly impact people's lives in ninety minutes on a Sunday morning and maybe a midweek service. New structures, new wineskins, new ideas must flood us by the power of the Holy Spirit. Again, I reference the cell group structure, which provides an excellent context for identifying needs, matching them with solutions and monitoring growth. Whether it is this or some other intentional model, the next generation will forge a place of healing and growth where the healing of the generations can take place, each one giving what the other lacks.

God will lead many men who have the Father's heart to begin to mentor young men in their congregations. As these godly fathers encounter young men interested in their fields of work, they will reach out and apprentice them. Older women will take the younger under their wings and impart love, nurture and wisdom. Strong families will reach out to single-parent homes and welcome ongoing interaction between the families, bringing strength and combatting the overwhelming sense of "aloneness." Creative ideas will abound for tutoring programs and classes on financial management. Teams will come together to assist other church members with home and automobile repairs. We will move toward the joy that the early church exuded as they lived in fellowship with each other and the Lord.

JEWISH/CHRISTIAN RECONCILIATION

At first glance it may seem redundant to raise this issue here when chapter 12 has been devoted to the Jewish roots of Christianity. However, there really are two separate issues with which we will deal.

The church is largely ignorant of the gross injustice and extreme hatred it has perpetrated toward Jewish people throughout most of church history. For the past one hundred years there has been an increased sensitivity toward and burden for Jewish people. For many of us, this is all we know. This time was preceded, however, by unspeakable acts of atrocity committed in the name of Christ, fueled by poisonous doctrine taught by some of the great theologians and church leaders of all time. Consider the following quote from a great church leader.

> What shall we do, we Christians do, with this damned, rejected race of Jews?...First, set fire to their synagogues and schools...Second, I advise that their houses also be razed and destroyed...Thirdly, I advise that all their prayer books...be taken from them...Fourth, I advise that rabbis be forbidden to teach henceforth on pain of loss of life and limb...Fifth, I advise that safe conduct on the highways be abolished completely for Jews...Sixth, I advise that all cash and...silver and gold be taken from them...Seventh, I recommend putting a flail, an axe, a hoe, a spade...in the hands of young, strong Jews and Jewesses, and letting them earn their bread by the sweat of their brow.[9]

Who said these terrible words? Was it someone from Hitler's Germany or a member of the Ku Klux Klan?

No, it was Martin Luther.

I urge you to take time to study the history of the church's interactions with the Jewish people. Books like Dr. Michael Brown's *Our Hands Are Stained With Blood* and many others show us the long, undeniable history of persecution and venom the institutional church has inflicted on these chosen people. John Dawson makes this comment:

> For nearly 2,000 years, parts of the Christian world relentlessly dehumanized the Jew. This helped pave the way for the Holocaust. Nazism was anti-Christian, but it gained part of its sustenance from the anti-Semitism that existed in Christendom.[10]

This generation must intentionally seek to reconcile this atrocious wrongdoing. Without agenda or secondary motive, we as a people must seek regular opportunities to seek the forgiveness of the Jewish people. This cannot be simply expressed toward the Messianic community, though certainly that is also valid. We must reach out to the Jewish community at large and actively bridge the gap of pain and separation that two thousand years of our hostility has brought.

THE MINISTRY OF RECONCILIATION

Recently I was with one of our groups in Israel, and we were touring the museum at David's Citadel. Our guide, a Jewish lady born in Israel, was doing a wonderful job explaining to us thousands of years of Jerusalem's history. When we entered the Crusader room, she began matter-of-factly describing the horrors of that time period and how it is recorded that the Crusaders massacred thousands of Jews and Muslims and then went to the Church of the Holy Sepulchre to offer thanks to God.

One of the people in our group, looking her square in the eye, said, "I am a Christian, and I want to tell you how sorry I am for what happened back then. These people were not properly showing forth Christ's love or His message."

"Oh, that is ancient history," our guide said. "You don't have to ask me to forgive you for anything."

At that point, a young lady intercessor from our group stepped up to her and said, "I am a Christian, and I am from Germany. I want to ask you to forgive me for what my nation has done to your people." The guide froze momentarily, shocked. Then she responded to the outstretched arms of the young German girl, and they embraced for several moments right there in the museum. And the true work of the cross, reconciliation of people to God and people to each other, came into that room.

What Now?

For group discussion:

1. All over the body of Christ right now we are being called to reconciliation. What dividing walls need to be broken down around you? Devote time to pursue this practically, whether in prayer or in action.

2. Where might repentance bring breakthrough around you? Would you consider repenting for your ancestors, your ethnic group or your church for its past or current sins?

3. What is one practical way your church could extend friendship to a church in your area from a different background? What about a joint Sunday service? A joint picnic? A combined evening of worship and music?

For personal application:

1. Consider any areas where prejudice could be present in your heart.

2. Take a morning and either alone or with a friend walk around an area where you are the only person or people of your ethnic background. Or visit a church on Sunday morning that is primarily of a different ethnic background. What does it feel like to be a minority?

3. Consider a way God could use you to bring healing and reconciliation to a situation you know is currently divided.

7

Spiritual Authority

*The next generation will have a mature
understanding of spiritual warfare. They will
begin to understand the interactions of the spirit realm
and be more adept at receiving help from angels
and resisting dark powers.*

Our ministry team of twenty-five was in the terminal of the Newark airport, headed to Israel for twelve days of worship and intercession during the Feast of *Shavuot* (Pentecost). I was traveling, as I often do, with my *shofar*, a trumpet made from a ram's horn. I had it wrapped around my arm.

Our flight had been delayed again and again. We had been waiting to board for nearly four hours. All over the room tensions were high as the gate area filled with Israelis trying to get home for the holiday. All of a sudden, over the loudspeaker the dreaded announcement came: Our flight had been canceled. We were being routed to the Sheraton for the night. Immediately, angry outbursts and expressions of frustration filled the terminal.

All of a sudden, out of the crowd a middle-aged Israeli in a blue-jean jacket strode right up to me. "You are the only one who can blow that shofar," he said in a thick Israeli accent, "and when you do, the atmosphere in here will change!"

I didn't know what to think of this, but almost instinctively, I lifted the shofar to my lips and let out a long blast. The terminal at the Newark airport grew silent, then all of a sudden erupted into a great cheer. Our team began to sing *"Hava Nagila,"* and soon, as amazing as it sounds, folks around us were clapping, singing with us and videotaping us! Talk about a change in the atmosphere!

Spiritual warfare is about changing the atmosphere. It is about declaring the lordship of Jesus in every arena in which we find ourselves!

There has been so much written on the subject of spiritual warfare, and I heartily recommend that the reader make use of the many excellent resources available. This chapter is not designed to give a comprehensive overview on the subject of spiritual warfare. We will simply point out this trend and offer some insights that may be helpful.

An increase in awareness of spirituality is evidenced everywhere. (See chapter 2.) Movies and TV shows with supernatural themes, New Age books, the incredible emphasis on angels—all of these point to our society's quest for contact with the spirit realm. Fears about everything from global economic collapse to nuclear war to unstoppable new super-viruses have mankind hoping that, somewhere out there, someone or something is watching out for us.

For believers, realization, emphasis and understanding of the spirit realm have increased dramatically in the past twenty years. However, I might comment that our realization and emphasis have outpaced our understanding.

The release of Frank Peretti's book *This Present Darkness* in 1989 is probably a good indicator of when the current national emphasis on spiritual warfare surfaced. Since then there has been an enormous increase of teaching on this subject—some of it good, some of it sensational and distracting.

I believe this next generation will sift through all that has been brought forth, "chew the meat, spit out the bones" and plunge into mature and effective warfare strategies necessary to fight the Lamb's war at the end of the age.

BASIC TRAINING

Let us lay a foundation by discussing the goal and the process of spiritual warfare.

- First of all, we must understand that *spiritual warfare is ultimately about lordship.*

All authority belongs to Christ. There is no domain free from the imposition of His sovereign will. God, in ways that often remain a mystery to mankind, traverses freely between man's moral will and His own divine sovereignty in the completion of His purposes for planet earth. There is no higher law than the law of His glorious love. It is important to remember that He is not just the God of the church, but the God of all the world. Every kingdom—finance, arts, education, government and so on—is being brought into subjection to His ultimate will and design. This will be done in a way that brings glory to the name of His Son and reveals the splendor and majesty of Jesus.

So when we talk about warfare, the *goal* of our warfare is not the battle, but the lordship of Christ we seek to bring to every domain. From the smallest to the greatest, every area is under His control (Col. 1:15–20). This begins with the revelation that all domains—companies, armies, universities, even nations—are run by mere people. These people all have an Achilles' heel—a point of vulnerability. Each of them need Christ! Jesus is not just after the domain. He deeply loves the souls who are working in it. He paid for them with His blood, and He wants them for His own.

All of a sudden our crusade to "clean up Hollywood" is broadened by an understanding that the people we may be tempted to vilify and demonize are hurting, broken people who need the love of Jesus. Our war against the spirit and practice of abortion is not just about that terrible act, but the doctors and nurses and mothers involved in this tragic choice. They too are victims of the lie of the enemy!

Our stance against the homosexual agenda moves beyond the cliché "hate the sin but love the sinner" to a deeper, more compassionate understanding of the pain and brokenness of that community. We offer deep repentance on behalf of our churches for what we have done, or not done, to contribute to that pain.

Our battle against New Age witchcraft moves beyond a paranoid fear of those practicing it to an understanding that they are people searching for truth and meaning.

We cannot—we must not—we dare not—see people as the "enemy." We are not wrestling against them. They are precious lives for whom Christ died. They have simply bought into a lie of the evil one—they are no different than we would be were it not for the grace of God. We learn that compassion, prayer and evangelism will introduce them to Jesus and bring His lordship to their kingdom.

- Second, we must understand that *the pathway to lordship is a process.*

We will spend the rest of our lives changing and growing into maturity in Christ. We must view our spiritual lives not as a goal, but as a process. We are committed to the long-term process of allowing the seed of the kingdom to take root and grow in us. This is especially necessary for those in leadership, where it is easy for our focus to shift from inward growth to outward ministry. Subconsciously we lose innocence and forward momentum in our personal walk with the Lord. We must actively resist self-righteousness, which was the downfall of the Pharisees. When we compare ourselves among one another, we are tempted to think, "I'm doing all right…I don't do this or that…My spiritual life is OK." But if we regularly spend moments in the presence of the holy God we will cry out with Isaiah, "Woe is me, for I am undone!" (Isa. 6:5, NKJV). We will genuinely feel our unholiness compared to His. We will be tempered with compassion and sensitivity because we will feel that we have received mercy.

We must not only be committed to growth and change, but we must also raise up a generation of believers who are committed to the ongoing, long-term process of becoming mature in Christ.

Our teaching and communication must change from salvation being an *experience* to salvation being a *lifestyle that begins with an experience.* Our children and our churches must begin to understand that we are called to "work out [our] salvation with fear and trembling" (Phil. 2:12), not simply pray a "fire insurance" prayer. The apostle Paul, a man who had tremendous revelation and unparalleled spiritual experience, had this understanding of being committed to the process. He shows this when he said he lived a life of discipline "so that after I have preached to others, I myself will not be disqualified for the prize" (1 Cor. 9:27).

- Third, we must recognize that *in order for the process to begin, breakthrough is often necessary.*

Those involved in any kind of addiction counseling are aware that until an addict hits "rock bottom"—until there is some drastic circumstance alarming enough to cause him to be desperate for change—then working toward change is probably futile. Our hearts are addicted to self and flesh, and our churches are addicted to mediocrity and lukewarmness. We will probably never truly begin the process toward lordship until we have a breakthrough, "rock bottom," shaking experience that causes us to cry out to God with holy desperation. The human desire for comfort is simply too strong to overcome without a radical jolt propelling us toward Him.

From individual hearts to local churches to cities, breakthrough is most often the first step toward change. If any substantive, foundational change is to occur, it will rarely come about gradually. Where strongholds exist in our personal lives, our churches or our communities, they will come in direct opposition and conflict to the lordship of Christ. The Lord Jesus will not tolerate "spot or wrinkle" in His bride, because He knows that ultimately she will be harmed by her compromise. (See Ephesians 5:27.) Moments of shaking—times that seem chaotic—are often necessary to expose the true state of affairs in the hearts of individuals, churches and people groups. Many times, trials or difficulties we label as "demonic" are completely allowed by the Lord in order to bring truth to the surface.

Character that is untested by the storms of adversity is not yet proven. Unity that is untested by the threat of division may be just surface cooperation. Maturity untested by difficult tribulation is not yet trustworthy. The Lord is after the *real thing.* He is looking for those whose hearts will not faint in the day of battle. Many times the first thing He will do to launch us forward on the road to *change* is to allow tumultuous, offensive circumstances to swirl around us. These divine tests, as Mike Bickle says, "offend the mind to reveal the heart."

ARENAS OF WARFARE

We can think of spiritual warfare in terms of three distinct arenas. They are *self, fields of entrustment* and *territories.* It is urgent that we understand that though these arenas are different, they are integrated and interrelated. It would be a drastic mistake to compartmentalize them and think that the activities of one are isolated from another.

Personal

Inner integrity brings spiritual authority. We must understand that spiritual warfare is not about special formulas or learning to "do it right." Spiritual warfare is about light replacing darkness, truth dethroning lies, freedom liberating bondage, love overcoming selfishness and life overcoming death. The beginning place in our battle training is here—in the chamber of our heart—where our affections and attitudes are seated.

It is dangerous to have more authority outwardly than inwardly. We will never have more authority than we have in our hearts. If we pretend that we do, it will destroy us and bring us down, as it has so many well-known ministries. The weight of the anointing will crush and break us if we do not deal with our own will and flesh, fully yielding ourselves to the Lord.

Relational Christianity, which we discussed in chapter 3, is vital. We are to grow in authority in the Lord. We must be intentional about having those chosen few around us those who know our struggles—our fears, our lusts, our pride. "God resists the proud, but gives grace to the humble" (James 4:6, NKJV). We will need much grace for the battle, and it is purchased with the currency of humility. We must be walking in the *process* that is taking us toward His lordship in every area of our lives.

Fields of entrustment

Fields of entrustment are things that the Lord has given you to steward. These are areas directly under your authority, or where you are part of a team that has authority over an area or a portion of an area.

For example, your family is an entrustment. A father is priest of the home and is responsible to the Lord for his impact on the family. Likewise, a mother moves in authority over her children while they are in the parents' home. Your physical dwelling place, your car, your bank account—these are items of stewardship the Lord has entrusted to you that He expects you to exercise dominion over. In all these areas you need to be committed to the process of bringing them under the lordship of Christ. This means evaluating what you allow into your home by way of television, videos, computers and music; it means evaluating how you spend your time and money; it means knowing the spiritual condition of your family.

Owning a business, leading a ministry, teaching in a school or university, holding a position in civic government—these are fields of entrustment. I believe that God gives you increased authority in the spirit realm as you pray over your employees or students, even if they are not believers. You bring the atmosphere, the presence of God, with you into the workplace. You realize that your interactions with people are part of the divine drama of the Lord drawing them to Himself.

Relationships are also fields of entrustment and spheres of influence God has given you with the people with whom you work, your neighbors, the people at the gym where you work out or the people at the post office you frequent. You are part of a divine drama being unfolded around you as you act as one of God's "secret agents" in this world, sowing the love and light of Jesus into every situation you encounter.

Territories

Third, I believe the Lord calls us into regional and territorial spiritual warfare. This begins with your city, state and nation. You are a representative of the kingdom of heaven in the midst of whatever other citizenship you hold. As priests who are called to "stand in the gap" on behalf of these territories, we cry out to God for mercy.

One example of this is found in Genesis 18 when the Lord is preparing to destroy Sodom and Gomorrah. The cup of judgment had been filled with the evil deeds of these cities and was about to be poured out upon them. Though he was not a resident of those cities, Abraham began a dialogue with God on their behalf. Abraham asked for, and received, assurances that if there were a righteous remnant present, the Lord would relent of the impending judgment. Abraham's nephew, Lot, should have been standing in intercession for those cities because he lived there. But he had been so ineffective in his witness that the cities were destroyed.

God is calling us, as never before, to invade our communities with light. This must happen in two ways. It must happen in extended times of worship and intercession, as we stand before the throne of grace and request mercy when we deserve judgment. It must also happen when we leave that place and become responsible, involved, caring people who make a difference as we live lives of authenticity and service to the people around us.

RESISTING SOULISH PRAYERS

As we are caught up in the emotion and intensity of praying for people, churches, situations or cities—anything that we feel deeply about—there comes a tendency to pray out of our own desire, even sometimes out of our own understanding, which to us seems godly. We have a natural tendency to assume that *self-preservation* and *avoidance of difficulty* must be God's will. We often fail to understand that God *allows* circumstances and wants to deliver us *in the midst of them,* but not necessarily *out of them.*

For example, can you imagine the intercessors for Shadrach, Meshach and Abednego? Can't you hear them even now, declaring the word of the

Lord over their lives, binding up the spirit of murder in the heart of the king, and canceling every assignment in the spirit realm against them that would put them into the fire (Dan. 3)? Or what about Daniel, being thrown into the lions' den (Dan. 6)? His intercessors would have been there declaring that the Lord would put a stop to it.

But in both of these and many other situations, God received *greater glory* by delivering His people in the midst of the trial, not delivering them from it. Is it wrong to resist the trial, bind up the enemy and so on? No, I think it is right to do those things, as long as we are doing them from the perspective that *our ultimate victory is not dependent on outward victory in this natural world.* The three Hebrew men were clear in their response to the king.

> Shadrach, Meshach and Abednego replied to the king, "O Nebuchadnezzar, we do not need to defend ourselves before you in this matter. If we are thrown into the blazing furnace, the God we serve is able to save us from it, and he will rescue us from your hand, O king. *But even if he does not,* we want you to know, O king, that we will not serve your gods or worship the image of gold you have set up."
>
> —DANIEL 3:16–18, EMPHASIS ADDED

The three Hebrews understood that even if the Lord did not deliver them from the furnace, they had not lost. Their faith would have stood the test, and they would have victoriously lived in truth in the midst of darkness. That was the real victory. Their physical lives were an important, but secondary matter.

Scripture records many others such as Isaiah and Stephen, who were martyred and yet died in faith. (See Acts 7:54–60.) Their victory was just as real and potent, though it was a victory evidenced on the other side of the veil. This next generation of intercessors and warriors will war for victory in natural circumstances, but be tempered with a mature understanding that the purposes that God is working in us and in His body are eternal and must be spiritually discerned and pursued.

Some attacks and pressures come solely for righteousness' sake, as in the case of Daniel and the others, but at other times they are allowed because the Lord is sifting and cleansing His people.

An excellent modern-day example of this is the life of Jim Bakker. While PTL was at the height of scandal, many intercessors and leaders there were desperately praying and acting out of a soulish concern for the ministry. Even if Bakker did sin, they thought the ministry as a whole was blessed of God and must remain. And so enormous spiritual and physical energy went into keeping the PTL "machine" going.

But God is sovereign, and God *did* allow PTL to crumble and allowed Bakker to endure an extremely harsh prison sentence. But look at the result! Today Jim Bakker stands as a humble, repentant leader voicing a clear word of the Lord to our generation to return to repentance and first love. He is ministering in the inner city of Los Angeles with his son, reaching out to the poorest of the poor in our nation. He is an example of brokenness and what the Lord can do when a person truly repents. Ultimately, God was not after PTL; God was after Jim Bakker's heart. Jesus died for people, not ministries.

Contrast this with other well-known ministries that have been rocked by scandal. They have not seen that in the midst of the attacks—some warranted and some not—that God was working an eternal purpose. Some of those ministries still have their ministry—at least the machine of it—but discernment makes it clear that there is little life or blessing of God on it.

Many times we pray from such a limited perspective and often even against the very thing the Lord is doing. "My ways [are] higher than your ways and my thoughts than your thoughts" (Isa. 55:9). We bring in our own perspectives and feelings into a situation and begin to pray out of that realm of thought rather than truly entering into the intercession of the High Priest, which is selfless and eternal.

For example, perhaps you are in a situation where there is division in your church or city. If you pray, especially in a group situation, "Lord, convict so-and-so of their sin and let them repent and stop dividing Your body," there are several problems you have reinforced that will distract you from the true purposes of the Lord.

You have put the focus of the prayer and the situation on an individual. This immediately counteracts our understanding that we are not warring against flesh and blood. You may be rightfully angry and the person indeed may be moving in falsehood, but the situation is not about one person. In focusing on flesh and blood, you switched to the wrong battlefield.

Your prayer is moving in the direction of the "accuser of the brethren" (Rev. 12:11). Whether the individual is wrong or not, he is still a child of God in need of love, mercy and forgiveness. God is fully able to bring judgment into their lives. We must not cry out for judgment for others while pleading for mercy for ourselves. Our stance as priests of the Lord is to cry out for mercy. To those unwilling to yield, His mercy comes in the form of judgment. But even His judgments are expressions of His mercy. We often cry out for judgment, but the Lord loves mercy.

> Do not gloat when your enemy falls; when he stumbles, do not let your heart rejoice, or the LORD will see and disapprove.
> —PROVERBS 24:17

If the Lord is instructing us to not gloat when our *enemy* falls, how much more compassion and empathy should we have with the body of Christ, our own brothers and sisters in Him!

PRAYING HIS WILL

Learn to pray and war, then, from a place of selflessness and humility, knowing that we "see through a glass, darkly" (1 Cor. 13:12, KJV). This does not undermine the force of our faith; rather it increases our firm belief that nothing can separate us from the love of God, and that the Lord does reign (Rom. 8:37–39).

Praying from the place of the Lord's Prayer is very powerful. "Thy kingdom come. Thy will be done" (Matt. 6:10, KJV). Declare confidently in every situation, no matter how difficult or painful, no matter how much shaking seems to be going on, that the will of the Lord shall prevail.

Remember that the devil is a created being and ultimately is a pawn in the hands of the Lord. God will cause good to come even out of evil. He will cause blessing to come even in the midst of the darkest situation.

WEAPONS OF WAR

The Lord has given us many weapons of war. We understand our spiritual armor from Ephesians. The following are some other weapons, or strongholds, that we must learn to utilize in battle. Francis Frangipane, in his excellent book *The Three Battlegrounds,* says that a stronghold is a "house made of thoughts."[1] This house of thoughts affects people individually and society corporately. For example, a person may be a racist, perhaps an anti-Semite. That is an individual stronghold. But that stronghold may spread to be a system of thought that infects entire peoples and regions, as it did in Nazi Germany.

In the same way, the people of God must learn to abide in the strongholds of the Lord. In this place of confident safety we are on the offensive, not the defensive, side of the battle. As the light of the Lord increases, the darkness of Satan's lies are pushed back.

WORSHIP

Worship is a powerful place, an atmosphere where much of the battle is waged individually and territorially. We will discuss this at length in chapter 11, "Restoring the Tabernacle of David."

BLESSING

The power of blessing is a lost weapon in much of the modern-day church. The laying on of hands and the speaking of blessing into an individual's life, or the blessing on a congregation, is more than nice words or a sentimental prayer. God's people have the authority in their fields of entrustment and spheres of influence to extend the power of blessing.

A blessing might go something like this:

Father, I thank You for my friend/son/wife/pastor. In Jesus' name, I bless them. I speak the blessing of Your strength, Your peace and Your power into their being. I thank You that they are covered in Your love and protected by Your blood. I thank You that You have blessed them with the mind of Christ and the fellowship of the Holy Spirit. I bless them, in Jesus' name, and thank You that Your protection is upon them, and they are covered with Your hands and sheltered in Your care.

Oftentimes the power of blessing can serve to realign the person being blessed with the truth. If we are always rebuking the enemy and "binding up" the attack coming against someone, our focus tends to be on the enemy and the attack rather than on what the positional blessing of the Lord is for those in Christ. I am not saying we should never rebuke the enemy or wage war in situations. I am simply saying that we might have to do less if we were, as priests of the Lord, more actively releasing the power of blessing on those around us.

Prophetic Declaration

A prophetic declaration is similar to a blessing but may be used in situations where there is less personal involvement, for example, over a city or church, or over people who are not yet believers.

When we declare something prophetically, we are simply agreeing with what we know is in the Word of the Lord. We are entering into the power of agreement with God's Word and declaring in faith what we do not yet see. "Now faith is the substance of things hoped for, the evidence of things not seen" (Heb. 11:1, NKJV).

So, for example, when I pray over New York City, I come as a priest before the Lord, knowing without question that one day, the "earth [including NYC] will be filled with the knowledge of the glory of the LORD, as the waters cover the sea" (Hab. 2:14).

So a prophetic declaration could be as follows:

Father, I thank You for my city/church/town/school. Thank You for making Your enemies Your footstool in this place (Ps. 110:1). I thank You that You are bringing every kingdom represented here into submission to the kingdom of Your Son, and that every knee will bow and every tongue confess that He is Lord. I release the angels of the Lord and the power of the Holy Spirit upon this place today. Have mercy on this place, and judge us in Your mercy and not Your wrath. I speak strength to my brothers and sisters in Christ throughout this place and declare that You are making us strong in the strength of the Lord that we might execute Your purposes and display Your glory.

Of course, these are just examples. What God is looking at even more than our words, is our hearts. He wants them to be filled with faith and the earnest expectation of His power being released.

THE FEAR OF THE LORD

The fear of the Lord is a huge, righteous stronghold that we have not dwelt in enough. The fear of the Lord is a living understanding and reality that God is bigger than our thoughts, abilities and understandings, and that any eternal impact or change is only going to come about through Him. The fear of the Lord comes when we genuinely enter into the living reality of the verse, "'Not by might nor by power, but by my Spirit,' says the LORD" (Zech. 4:6).

I was in a meeting once where a number of pastors and leaders were discussing a major missions project that needed to be undertaken. It involved a great deal of natural work and, potentially, a great deal of spiritual warfare. We had identified a vast and consuming need, but we did not know how the need would be filled.

One of the pastors there from a very large church spoke up and said in a very lighthearted and flippant tone, "Well, we'll just take care of it. Our church can handle this." Everyone present knew that this church, in the natural, had the resources to deal with this situation, and so the conversation took its course, assuming that this is what we would do.

Inwardly I groaned as this unfolded—not because of what the pastor said, but because of the attitude in which it was expressed. "Sure, we can handle it"—the words revealed a natural reliance on his church's ability rather than expressing a sense of burden or the leading of the Lord in accepting the assignment.

The fear of the Lord is the attitude James was referring to when he urged us to speak in humility about our plans for the future.

> Now listen, you who say, "Today or tomorrow we will go to this or that city, spend a year there, carry on business and make money." Why, you do not even know what will happen tomorrow. What is your life? You are a mist that appears for a little while and then vanishes. Instead, you ought to say, "If it is the Lord's will, we will live and do this or that."
>
> —James 4:13–15

So many times we naturally gravitate toward that which seems good and easily attainable through our own efforts. We fail to wait on the Lord for His best plan or leave room for His Holy Spirit to surprise us with His strategy. Looking back over my years in ministry, I see so many times where I moved out in what seemed like a good idea to me, even convincing myself that it was the Lord "opening a door," only to realize later the futility and lack of results when I move in my own strength. Likewise, I can see times when I did wait on the Lord and accessed His wisdom, and I marveled at how He took situations that seemed impossible and supernaturally turned them around.

The Goodness of the Lord

The key area of warfare, the key battleground, is where the enemy strives to make us doubt the goodness of God. Satan wants us to doubt that God is good—that He really loves us and is for us. Faith in the goodness of God keeps seeds of doubt and discouragement from being planted and being effective against us.

This began in the garden.

> Now the serpent was more crafty than any of the wild animals the
> LORD God had made. He said to the woman, "Did God really say,
> 'You must not eat from any tree in the garden'?" The woman said to
> the serpent, "We may eat fruit from the trees in the garden, but God
> did say, 'You must not eat fruit from the tree that is in the middle of
> the garden, and you must not touch it, or you will die.'" "You will
> not surely die," the serpent said to the woman. "For God knows that
> when you eat of it your eyes will be opened, and you will be like
> God, knowing good and evil."
>
> —GENESIS 3:1–5

The essence of the first temptation was that Satan caused Eve to
believe that God was not truly good, that God was holding out on her,
keeping from her something that would really be beneficial.

This is still the root of temptation today and the crux of all warfare.
The enemy whispers lies to us, urging us to sin, to give in to our flesh, to
believe that God really isn't good and His ways aren't best.

When Satan cannot get to us with blatant sin, he will cause us to be
worn out through constant questioning. "What good has it done that you
have served God? What has it gained you that you have been righteous?
You have the same troubles and trials as anyone else. If God is really
there, why hasn't He cared for you?"

David faced this temptation as he looked at evil men around him.

> For I envied the arrogant when I saw the prosperity of the wicked.
> They have no struggles; their bodies are healthy and strong. They
> are free from the burdens common to man; they are not plagued
> by human ills. Therefore pride is their necklace; they clothe them-
> selves with violence. From their callous hearts comes iniquity; the
> evil conceits of their minds know no limits. They scoff, and speak
> with malice; in their arrogance they threaten oppression. Their
> mouths lay claim to heaven, and their tongues take possession of

the earth. Therefore their people turn to them and drink up waters in abundance. They say, "How can God know? Does the Most High have knowledge?" This is what the wicked are like—always care-free, they increase in wealth. Surely in vain have I kept my heart pure; in vain have I washed my hands in innocence. All day long I have been plagued; I have been punished every morning. If I had said, "I will speak thus," I would have betrayed your children. When I tried to understand all this, it was oppressive to me...

—PSALM 73:3–16

How did David combat this discouragement? How did he overcome this stronghold attacking his mind and heart, urging him to forget about God and His ways? *He ran to the stronghold!*

...till I entered the sanctuary of God; then I understood their final destiny.

—PSALM 73:17

David set his gaze on the One he loved, the Lord, his stronghold. He came away from the lies and noise of the enemy and wrestled until his heart was past the outer court of religious activity and into the holy place of God's presence. There, in that place of abandonment to his eternal friend, he found the comfort of the Lord's embrace.

Yet I am always with you; you hold me by my right hand. You guide me with your counsel, and afterward you will take me into glory. Whom have I in heaven but you? And earth has nothing I desire besides you. My flesh and my heart may fail, but God is the strength of my heart and my portion forever. Those who are far from you will perish; you destroy all who are unfaithful to you. But as for me, it is good to be near God. I have made the Sovereign LORD my refuge; I will tell of all your deeds.

—PSALM 73:23–28

As David laid hold of this truth personally, so the children of Israel laid hold of it corporately. While marching to battle against their enemies, the battle song the Lord gave them did not speak of His might or His power or their past victories. Instead they sang of their unfailing confidence in His goodness and mercy.

> After consulting the people, Jehoshaphat appointed men to sing to the LORD and to praise him for the splendor of his holiness as they went out at the head of the army, saying: "Give thanks to the LORD, for his love endures forever." As they began to sing and praise, the LORD set ambushes against the men of Ammon and Moab and Mount Seir who were invading Judah, and they were defeated.
>
> —2 CHRONICLES 20:21–22

As these End-Times days approach, and the earth shakes and judgment falls, we must run to the stronghold called the Goodness of the Lord and become unshakeable in our belief that whatever may come, God is good. Individually and corporately, this will be one of our primary weapons of war. In a time when "men's hearts [are] failing them for fear," we will have confidence the Lord is in complete control and is arranging every circumstance according to His plan and purpose (Luke 21:26, KJV).

STEWARDSHIP AND GIVING

Another powerful weapon in the hands of believers is the power of money. God calls us to two types of warfare in this arena—stewardship and giving. Unfortunately, Western Christianity has been so exploited in this area that we have shied away from this truth, fearing if we talk about finance we will be labeled as money hungry. But the fact remains that God does command us to tithe and, beyond that, encourages us to give. If we are to be prepared for the days of economic instability that many spiritual and secular leaders are saying are soon upon us, then we need to sow much seed into the kingdom of God.

> He who is kind to the poor lends to the LORD, and he will reward
> him for what he has done.
>
> —PROVERBS 19:17

God is urging us to give personally to those we know are in need and then to credible, established ministries who are committed to being a blessing to the poor of the earth. I think of this as a spiritual bank account. Every time I give, I am making a deposit. The Lord sees this and rewards those who are generous.

As we are careful with our finances and live within our means, resisting the American urge toward debt, we are freed from yokes and pressures that a focus on material things brings. Simplifying our lifestyles brings us to a place of contentment as we focus on the inner life of the kingdom, and the enemy has less and less room to vex us in these arenas.

FINALLY...

We are learning much as the body of Christ these days, understanding more and more how to discern the schemes of the enemy and abide in the Lord, our protector, for strength and wisdom. The next generation will deepen its understanding of discernment as they prepare to serve and obey as soldiers in the last-days battle. The Lord is clothing us with His zeal and anointing us with His name. In the Old Testament, every time the Lord revealed His name (*Jehovah-Shalom,* the Lord our peace; *Jehovah-Rapha,* the Lord our healer), He revealed an aspect of His character. We are confronting the enemy in the name—the character—of the Lord Jesus Christ. When we come, it is not His spoken name that is a talisman or good luck charm. It is His name in us, His character being worked in and through us, that assures us of victory. Like David, we are not relying on Saul's armor, the arm of the flesh, but coming against the forces of this world's kingdoms in the strength of the name of the Lord. (See 1 Samuel 17:38–40.)

What Now?

For group discussion:

1. What spheres of influence has God given your group, and how is He calling you to steward that influence?

2. The Lord has given us many weapons of war (for example, worship, blessing and prophetic declaration). Discuss these weapons and how to utilize them in a biblical way.

3. Read Ephesians 6:8–10; notice that Paul is telling us to prepare for war. Discuss the elements of a Christian walk in this world and in the Spirit that are warlike, and how we can be a strengthened, sharpened weapon for God.

For personal application:

1. What spheres of influence has God given you, and how is He calling you to steward that influence?

2. Identify strongholds, or houses of thought, that you know you need to stand against in your own life and the lives of your family members.

3. The Word teaches us that there is power in united prayer. Come together with a prayer partner and commit to praying together regularly until you see breakthrough in an area for which you have a burden.

8

The Citywide Family of God

The next generation will embrace the concept of the "City Church." They will think of the church along city and regional terms and begin to see their local church as one expression of the church of Jesus Christ in the city.

Rick Ridings is a respected leader in the prayer movement, whose ministry has taken him all over the world. He shares a vision that properly sets the stage for this chapter.

A VISION OF AMERICA'S CITIES

As I was interceding one day for American cities in 1990, I saw a vision that I have not widely shared until now [Fall, 1993]. I have shared this vision with brothers whom I respect and trust such as Jack Hayford and John Dawson. They told me they felt the vision was from the Lord and that they saw it as being in line with what they feel God is desiring to say to the cities of America. I now submit it to a broader portion of the body of Christ to consider prayerfully:

In the vision, I saw trumpets sounding the same message in every direction. They were calling upon suburban American churches to put a priority upon praying for their city and to receive God's heart of compassion for the enormous needs of the inner city. They were calling suburban churches to build bridges of love and relationship to inner-city churches, bridges characterized by genuine friendships between leaders and congregations rather than any sense of paternalism.

The cities all had a pool in the very center of them. In certain cities, the suburban churches laid aside certain activities in order to give themselves to obeying the call of the trumpets. As they did, the pool in the center of each of these cities turned into crystal clear water and shot up as a great fountain. The fountain cascaded out over the suburbs and surrounding areas. Wherever the water fell, immediately there sprang up beautiful flowers, which quickly turned into magnificent fruit.

In other cities, I saw the leaders of suburban churches plugging their ears and saying, "We just don't have time to do all that. We're too busy with all of our present programs, and we can't stop any of them." In those cities, the pool in the center turned into a pool of vomit. It too sprang up into a fountain. And everywhere the vomit fell, flames sprang up, which quickly burnt everything they touched until there were only ashes left.

As I considered and prayed about this, I felt God was saying that America would not experience across-the-board judgment or revival. Rather, certain cities that respond to God's widespread prophetic call will experience revival, starting where they least expected it, in the inner cities. Other cities, by contrast, will experience judgment. But this time the burning and destruction will not be contained in the inner cities, but will spread to engulf the so-called "safe suburbs."

What is the criteria for moving on into revival and escaping judgment? Simply adjusting church life to reflect God's agenda and priorities at this time: praying for the whole of our city, receiving His heart of compassion for the inner city and seeking to build bridges of genuine friendships between leaders of suburban and inner-city churches.[1]

UNITY

How good and pleasant it is when brothers live together in unity...For there the LORD bestows His blessing, even life forevermore.

—PSALM 133:1, 3

My prayer is not for them alone. I [Jesus] pray also for those who will believe in me through their message, that all of them may be one, Father, just as you are in me and I am in you.

—JOHN 17:20–21

It is clear that the Lord places high importance on unity. John 17 is the last recorded prayer of Jesus before He went to the cross, and in that desperate time He lifted His request to the Father that we would be one. Notice the level and quality of unity He prays for. It is not a superficial cooperation or status quo peaceful interaction. He prays that we, the body of Christ, would move in the same level and quality of unity that He and the Father move in.

I believe that one key to this unity is found in the above psalm in the words *dwell together.*

Most churches and leaders, even if they are "independent" churches, have some denominational or relational context to which they relate. These affiliations are based on denominational background, educational institution or doctrinal persuasion. Leaders travel great distances for annual national conferences or councils. They also travel perhaps an hour or so on a monthly or quarterly basis to meet with their "district," "section" or "conference."

All too many times, however, they don't even know the pastors and leaders within a ten-mile radius of their church's front door.

That is changing!

A THEOLOGY OF THE CITY

Throughout Scripture God is seen interacting with people on all different levels. He deals with individuals, tribes, nations, families and very often, with cities. Cities are seen not only as the building blocks of nation-states, but also as independent entities in themselves with their own spiritual climate. From Genesis to Revelation, blessing and cursing, judgment or protection, are granted to cities, depending on their righteousness or lack thereof.

The first mention of God's dealing with a city in Scripture is in Genesis 18, when the Lord speaks to Abraham regarding Sodom and Gomorrah. God's conversation with Abraham here helps to reveal how He views cities.

> When the men got up to leave, they looked down toward Sodom, and Abraham walked along with them to see them on their way. Then the LORD said, "Shall I hide from Abraham what I am about to do?"
>
> —GENESIS 18:16–17

It is a rhetorical question. In other words, God said, "I will tell Abraham my plans."

> Abraham will surely become a great and powerful nation, and all nations on earth will be blessed through him. For I have chosen him, so that he will direct his children and his household after him to keep the way of the LORD by doing what is right and just, so that the LORD will bring about for Abraham what he has promised him.
>
> —GENESIS 18:18–19

We see in verse 17 that Abraham had entered into a relationship with God that brought about revelation. *Relationship* brings *revelation*. As one of the righteous who lived in the general region of Sodom and Gomorrah and someone who had family there, Abraham was granted access to divine information.

In the same way, this generation will begin to know the thoughts and mind of the Lord for their cities. It is a good thing to have a burden for our nation, but our nation is made up of cities. Thinking, acting and praying in terms of cities provide measurable, definable battlefields for a confrontation with forces of darkness. You can map out a city, identify the churches, see what areas are especially plagued with violence, witchcraft or other ills.

WHO IS CRYING OUT?

The next thing the Lord revealed is very interesting.

> Then the LORD said, "The outcry against Sodom and Gomorrah is so great and their sin so grievous that I will go down and see if what they have done is as bad as the outcry that has reached me. If not, I will know."
>
> —GENESIS 18:20–21

Who was crying out against these cities? Surely not the Lord, since He was the one going to investigate the cries. And since we later see that there are practically no righteous in the cities, it cannot be the prayers of the saints crying out. Who, or what, then, was crying out against Sodom and Gomorrah?

These cries point to the spiritual realities behind physical actions. The sinful acts being committed there were causing a cloud of complaint to come up before the Lord. We see that physical activities, both sinful and righteous, create a cry in the spirit realm that is recognized by spiritual forces. Look at the scriptural account of the first murder.

> Then the LORD said to Cain, "Where is your brother Abel?" "I don't know," he replied. "Am I my brother's keeper?" The LORD said, "What have you done? Listen! *Your brother's blood cries out to me from the ground.*"
>
> —GENESIS 4:9–10, EMPHASIS ADDED

Notice how the verse said the land reacted to the sin that took place upon it. Here's another similar example.

Even the land was defiled; so I punished it for its sin, and the land vomited out its inhabitants. But you must keep my decrees and my laws. The native-born and the aliens living among you must not do any of these detestable things, for all these things were done by the people who lived in the land before you, *and the land became defiled. And if you defile the land, it will vomit you out as it vomited out the nations that were before you.*

—LEVITICUS 18:25–28, EMPHASIS ADDED

We must realize that the murder, abortion, molestation and all manner of sin committed in our cities have an impact far beyond the lives of the victims, as tragic as their pain is. I believe there is scriptural basis for believing that sin emits a cloud of darkness and stench in the spirit realm over cities. Sin literally affects the spiritual climate, or spiritual atmosphere. Thus, our response against sin must not simply be anger at the perpetrators, pity for the victims and fear for ourselves. These are all simply emotional, human responses. Our spiritual response as priests of the Lord must be to stand in identificational repentance for the sins of the city, crying out to the Lord for mercy and cleansing.

FOR THE SAKE OF FIFTY

When the Lord went down to consider the outcry against Sodom and Gomorrah, He was looking for a presence of the righteous.

The LORD said, "If I find fifty righteous people in the city of Sodom, I will spare the whole place for their sake."

—GENESIS 18:26

A famous dialogue follows in which Abraham intercedes with the Lord on behalf of these cities. The Lord is seen here as one who dialogues with the intercessors. His heart is not to destroy but to save; however, repentance is necessary. This and other scriptural accounts, such as the repentance of the city of Nineveh, counteract a doomsday mentality that it is too late for our cities or nations. Too many preachers give an incessant cry of destruction, which leans toward fatalism. They contradict scriptural principles that show God loves mercy and urges all men to repent. Judgment may come to a nation, but certain cities may be spared. Judgment may come to a city, but certain sections and neighborhoods may be spared. For example, in the midst of the destruction of Egypt, Goshen rested in the safety of the Lord (Exod. 7–12). While we have voices to raise to God and cry out for mercy, there is hope.

OUR VOICE IS LOUDER

There are also clear scriptural precedents that show that God's blessing resides over cities where there is a strong history or presence of righteousness. While sin brings a clouded atmosphere of death to a city or territory, acts of righteousness push back the darkness, tearing open the veil of the enemy and allowing for an open heaven for God's blessings.

There are many offerings to the Lord that produce this climate change: Intercession, repentance, prayerwalking, worship (which we will cover extensively in chapter 11), ministry to the poor, prophetic declaration. All of these are needed, but there is one strategy that I believe is extremely potent and is gaining understanding in our day. It is the power of the Psalm 133 blessing—the unity of the elders in the city.

THE CRUCIBLE OF RELATIONSHIPS

We don't grow in a vacuum. Our whole life is made up of interaction with people—family, friends, classmates, coworkers. Our interaction with people strongly shapes and influences everything about us—how we dress, worship, communicate, eat and live.

Likewise, the body of Christ does not mature in a vacuum. The body requires a context, a place in which to grow and mature in faith. For most of us, this is our local church. It is the place we learn, serve, are discipled and in turn, disciple others.

Leaders, however, often have a daunting challenge to find a place for continued spiritual growth. Often, four to six years are given to a Bible college or seminary education, and from there they head right into ministry. Right or wrong, the unalterable fact is that people place upon leaders expectations that are hard to meet! Leaders are required to evidence a certain level of spiritual strength and emotional stability. The unstated but underlying message to leaders is, "Hey, you had better have your act together because that's what you get paid for. If you have doubts, problems or pains, you had better not let the people see them, or they might lose faith, and you might lose your job." These are rarely said in these terms, of course, but the reality is that pastors and church leaders are among the loneliest people because so often they cannot find a context for encouragement, personal growth, accountability and healing.

Denominations and fellowships are supposed to provide this, and perhaps in a small measure they do. But it is extremely unrealistic to maintain vital, life-building relationships with people miles and hours away that you see monthly or even just yearly.

God is now breathing on this nation with a fresh wind from heaven, and a phenomenon is taking place. All across America local pastors are finding one another. Relational networks are springing up everywhere with no agenda other than to worship to God and find friendship with one another. These are not the typical ministerial associations, which are generally more formal and event driven. Rather, these are loose, friendship-based networks that come together—some weekly, some monthly—simply to worship the Lord and spend time growing in friendship with one another. There is no umbrella organization sponsoring or monitoring this, although surely there is a debt of gratitude owed to organizations like March for Jesus, Concerts of Prayer, and others. This is simply a work of the Holy Spirit where pastors and leaders are finding walls crumbling and genuine affection and care for one another.

One city really beginning to enjoy this type of unity is Harrisburg, Pennsylvania. Several years ago, a handful of pastors began to get together for prayer and fellowship. As the Lord smiled on their times together, the fellowship became sweet and a genuine sense of encouragement began to mark their meetings. Their number grew until dozens of pastors from across denominational and racial lines were meeting regularly, seeking God's blessing and strategy for their individual and corporate ministry.

A day came when they had an opportunity for a dramatic declaration of the unity of the church in their city. Geographically, Harrisburg is divided by the river that flows through its center. The geographic division, however, marked a racial and socio-economic one as well. The two sides of the city on the two sides of the river were very divided. But this group of city leaders brought their church together, and in a demonstration of unity, thousands of believers joined hands and crossed this bridge and met in the middle. Then the body of Christ in Harrisburg went down to the river and baptized more than two hundred believers that day.

If you are not a pastor, this may not sound all that revolutionary to you. But if you are in full-time ministry, you know what a miracle it is to grow true relationship between pastors in a city!

Why is this so crucial? Because God is after our cities! And if we are going to reverse the curse and take our cities for God, it is not going to be our denominational acquaintance forty miles away who is going to take it with us. *God will not deliver a city to a local church or local pastor— though He often uses one local church and leader as a catalyst. God will deliver a city to His body in that city—Pentecostal, evangelical, Messianic, mainline, white, black, Asian. It will take the whole body to win the whole city.* No matter how wonderful your ministry or your church is, I believe God will never fully deliver a city to a church, pastor, evangelist or ministry. The temptation to pride and self-glory would be too great. He will use anointed individuals as catalysts to galvanize a citywide move, but those individuals will have a deep commitment to team ministry and naturally share leadership with the key individuals God raises up.

Pastor Joseph Garlington states this point frequently when he speaks:

The thing of which I am a part is greater than the part I play.

These relationships are not easy! Developing this type of true spiritual family among Christian leaders in a city is desperately hard work. But the end result will be a new, higher quality of Christian life for believers in your entire city and a people prepared for the greatest harvest of souls the world has ever seen.

FIVE HARD STEPS TO TERRITORIAL AUTHORITY

Here are five steps, or phases, that I believe citywide elderships need to go through in order to reach a mature level of spiritual authority in a territory.

1. *Intentionality*

The first step toward relationship must be an intentional commitment. Someone, somewhere, somehow has to make a first step toward building the relationships.

Many times these networks begin simply as a time of prayer once a week. You do not need many to start with the Lord's presence in your midst. "Where two or three are gathered...I am there" (Matt. 18:20, NKJV). Your citywide network does not have to start out with a dozen leaders. In many cases, it is better that it not. If it starts too large, it will be less able to be relaxed. It is best if it is built on a nucleus of a few praying elders who simply make a commitment to pray and encourage one another regularly.

This kind of network will grow. It will not grow by strategy or program, but it will grow naturally as others are welcomed in through the doorway of relationship. Some will come regularly—others occasionally. Eventually it will be easy to identify the core group that will maintain a real commitment to the relationships. The Lord could produce this suddenly or, more likely, over several years. Eventually this network will lead to a measure of...

2. *Trust*

Once there is a sense of commitment and a level of camaraderie, the relationships will move from professional alliances to genuine friendships. Discussion will move from Sunday's service to more heartfelt issues, like family or personal goals and projects. At this crucial stage, the relationships must move deeper. Perhaps you go away to a retreat or conference together for a few days. Maybe you do a pulpit exchange, or you begin to fellowship in each other's homes. Fellowshiping with someone in their home is inviting them into a part of your life. You begin to know one another's family members, church situations and other touch points of concern. Masks will begin to come down, and genuine empathy will be present in the relationships. This will open the doorway for…

3. Repentance

At this point, true repentance leading to change can begin to flow. This repentance will happen at a number of levels. Sources of contention between leaders will surface—old hurts and bitterness over church splits, competition, overheard comments, people who have transferred from one church to another, misperceptions. These will be confessed and turned away from. Then, also, individual struggles can be confessed—anger, marital strife and so on. Finally, the pastor or leader has a safe place to confess faults one to another and find healing. Pride and the keeping-up-of-appearances are subdued, and the blessing of humility and brotherly love take their place. This allows the city elders to move into a place of…

4. Honesty

Things move much quicker now. Trust has been established as a firm foundation, and honesty fills meetings and prayer times. The energy of truth cleans the atmosphere. The relationships move to a place of understanding each other's temperments and personalities. Because they understand one another now, they release each other into who they are in their individual strengths, not worrying that one individual is self-promoting. Honest questions can be voiced without fear, and honest answers given. The dynamic of synergy—"a release of efficiency born from releasing individuals into their strengths and giftings"—comes to their midst. They realize that they are stronger together than apart. Truth always brings freedom, and a great sense of freedom marks the relationships, which are well on their way to biblical…

5. *Unity*

Biblical unity. Not cooperation or participation, but true unity—the same quality of unity that God the Father and Jesus share. That is the kind of unity Jesus prayed we would have. His prayer will be answered. We don't even really know what that quality of unity feels like yet. It is a unity that prefers others over ourselves; considers the cause of the kingdom over our own needs; is free from selfish ambition and impure motives. We have not yet drunk the air cleansed by the Psalm 133 blessing on unity, where God commands "life forevermore." But we will.

And as this quality of unity rises in the body of Christ, we will see a release of....

AUTHORITY

We have not yet begun to touch the level of authority in all realms that will be released to the church of Jesus Christ when we come to this level of kingdom unity. I believe in the realm of the natural we will see governmental officials coming to the church for answers to societal problems like illiteracy, homelessness and drugs. Imagine the authority we will possess when we speak to the school boards of this nation with a united voice, representing thousands. Politicians will no longer be able to run from church to church, seeking favor from single, influential pastors. The city church will possess incredible influence on civic affairs. We will move as one man with unprecedented strength and be, finally, a powerful example and witness of the love and life of Christ.

In the supernatural realm, keys of authority will be released. In the context of the unified relationships of these city elders we will find the authority to enact executive, legislative prayer over cities and territories. This prayer will be powerful and effective, and will produce measurable results, such as Elijah's prayer that dictated the weather.

Genuine healings of biblical proportions will take place. No Christian celebrity or superstar will get the recognition, but the elders of the city will be used and Jesus' name alone will be glorified.

IF WE BUILD IT, HE WILL COME

I sat recently with a Christian leader who had just returned from hosting a spiritual warfare conference. I asked how the conference went, and he replied, "It was good, but it seems we did not have a true breakthrough. I feel there is a real anointing over this city waiting to be released, but for some reason it is being held back."

I happen to minister a great deal in this particular city and work with several churches. I am in good relationship with many of the pastors. This leader only works with one church in that city—the largest church. I happen to know he has never taken the time to hear any perspective or receive any input from the other pastors. How can this conference seek a citywide breakthrough when it is only going through one gate?

I appreciate the pastor of this large church. I minister there and have an excellent relationship with him. Frankly, I believe that God has ordained him as *a,* if not *the,* significant elder in that city. *But we will never have citywide, territorial breakthrough if we are only going through one gate.* God deeply loves and is completely committed to all His faithful servants throughout the city. He will not simply show up at one place and expect all the other faithful leaders to be only recipients and spectators, or have token recognition. No, these other pastors and leaders throughout the city have invested years of prayer and faithfulness into the heavenly realm, and the Lord will see that they are rewarded as well. He will simply not rest His glory in one house with one gatekeeper.

I know many might say that the current movements in Pensacola, Florida, and Toronto would seem to prove otherwise, but I think a closer examination shows otherwise. The grace and blessing of God has clearly been on these churches, but their impact, while powerful, has actually been more national and international than it has been local. Both churches are drawing believers from hundreds and even thousands of miles away to seek more of God. However, our prayers must desire that these revivals translate into long-term, whole-scale societal impact for the regions of Pensacola and Toronto. God is after more than wells to which people can travel and be refreshed, as wonderful as that is. But God is desirous that we, His people, work to possess the gates of our own cities and see the atmosphere literally changed with an infusion of holy light.

The Lord is waiting for us to form citywide wineskins into which He can pour fresh wine, oil and fire to take our cities. Stop seeking the Lord for "your" church. It is not "your" church—it is His. And His church is not your local expression of it. It is the church of the city.

We have tried to engage the enemy on his own territory and lost miserably. The beginning place for national revival resulting in societal impact is simple. Pastors, leaders, elders in the body of Christ in individual cities must come into biblical unity. It is there God "bestows his blessing, even life forevermore" (Ps. 133:3).

What Now?

~

1. Discuss the current state of the unity of churches in your city. Does it seem unified? What is practical evidence of this?

2. Are there churches or ministries with which your group has an ongoing relationship? In what ways can God's church in your region be more unified, and what part can you play in that?

3. Consider working toward a night of worship and intercession where you could gather intercessors from all over the area to meet in a neutral site for a "church of the city" event.

For personal application:

1. List the churches you drive by regularly on the way to your church. Find out the pastors' names and something about those churches to begin lifting them up in prayer as you pass them.

2. Consider jotting a thank-you note or sending a small gift to a pastor or spiritual leader in your area. Find practical ways to encourage those who are serving the Lord in ministry.

3. Find out about March for Jesus, Concerts of Prayer or other similar regional events happening in your area and get involved.

9

Abiding in the Secret Place

The next generation will embrace the value of the quiet place.

I was once in Honduras with a missionary friend of mine, Jonathan Smoak, who does extensive traveling around the world, especially to places of great darkness and desperation. While walking through a very poor rural village, just outside the capital city of Tegucigalpa, we talked about the vast differences between a typical day for a villager and a typical day for a middle-class American. As we were talking he turned to me and asked, "Do you know what the definition of poverty is?" I thought of many things like lack of water, lack of food or even lack of money. He listened to all my ideas and then soberly responded, "No. The definition of poverty is very simply—lack of options."

That definition has impacted my life as I think about its implication on the spiritual vitality of the church in America. What is a primary characteristic of the modern Western world? Abundance of options. What is the primary stumbling block that keeps so much of the West in a place of spiritual immaturity? Abundance of materialistic options.

UNHEALTHY SOULS

Today in the West there is a soul-wrenching cry for reality and significance. Though the increase of technology's gadgets, devices and opportunities has resulted in higher standards of living, there seems to be a decrease in people's ability to enjoy life. People have falsely assumed that their blessings of options would increase their happiness, contentment and sense of significance. *But with the blessing of options has also come the curse of distraction.*

The wealth of the West has created a society with a lingering cloud of tempting distractions. Because our society offers many options, people have filled up their time with more and more things in hope that they would find satisfaction and joy. The result is that people are busier than ever—busy from pursuing so many distractions. The hard reality is that it takes time to live, and real living means taking time to cultivate the health of one's soul. *The issue is not just about having distractions. It's about most people in our society having learned lifestyles of distractions where they lose the ability simply to be and cannot find meaning and joy apart from the toys and accruements of modern life.* Such inability is the result of an unhealthy soul.

WHAT IS THE QUIET PLACE?

The quiet place is not merely a place one goes to as much as it is a condition or a way of living that Christ is seeking to build into our lives. It is that place of internal stillness and rest within the soul of the believer where he or she has learned the discipline of focused listening. In this place the believer is not distracted by all the voices of the world or even those of self, for such a one has learned to hear God above everything else. If we do not learn to live out of the quiet place we will inevitably succumb to living out of the place of frantic busy-ness from all the whirlwinds of schedule and agenda. Only in this place is where we hear the voice of God and know His fellowship. The quiet place must be actively pursued or it will get crowded out of our lives. Yet the ongoing building of this condition in our lives requires a deliberate choice to get away to a physically quiet and serene location. A practical application for a tangible quiet place is found in commitment to the Sabbath principle.

DISTRACTIONS OF NECESSITIES

In twentieth-century life, distractions of *necessities* and distractions of *options* are constantly vying for people's attention. By distractions of necessities I refer to all those choices that face us in our times of work and responsibility—choices of necessity. No longer can we simply go into the consumer market and buy groceries, clothes, appliances, vehicles or whatever things are needed. We must make decisions from among a multitude of choices and brands. So it seems as if we are ever trying to live but never able to slow down enough to enjoy it. Not only do we have to deal with choices as an informed consumer, but we also have to deal with the smorgasbord of choices that the very nature of our affluent society affords us. A vacation doesn't just mean time away from work. A vacation requires charting out an agenda of what to do and where to go. Affluent societies afford such options.

DISTRACTION OF OPTIONS

By distraction of *options* I refer to all those choices that face us in our times away from work and responsibility—choices of leisure. When people are able to find time outside of their necessary functions and duties, they easily get sucked into investing their time and energies into things that bring immediate satisfaction and thrill. There are simply so many more "thrilling" and "exciting" options available that never were there before. As a result, people neglect their souls by focusing so much on the gratification of the senses of their bodies.

We must learn to become ruthless with choosing those things that make for the health of our souls if we desire to experience a measure of meaning and significance in our lives. Central to such health are the factors of simplicity and quietness. Just as we have learned to live lifestyles of distraction, so too must we learn to live lifestyles of simplicity and quietness. Such actions are injections of health to our souls in a very unhealthy society.

Richard Foster in *Freedom of Simplicity* comments, "Contemporary culture is plagued by the passion to possess. The unreasoned boast abounds that the good life is found in accumulation, that 'more is better.' Indeed, we often accept this notion without question, with the result that the lust for affluence in contemporary society has become psychotic: it has completely lost touch with reality.... The complexity of rushing to achieve and accumulate more and more frequently threatens to overwhelm us; it seems there is no escape from the rat race."[1]

RETHINKING OUR CHOICES

What are we being distracted from? We are distracted from paying closer attention to, and placing greater investment in, the divinely ordained "well" of simple contentment. God has placed this well in the soul of every man and woman. Our complexity and speed of life have caused us to become deaf to the rhythm and harmony of life that our Creator has made us to enjoy. Our choices and pace of life have often tended to clutter and confuse us in our journey more than deliver the virtues of contentment and happiness so ardently sought. As society becomes increasingly aware that its lifestyles and options are not bringing the satisfaction it desires, frustration results. People's frustrations are causing them either to try harder or try again. Many people are not willing simply to try harder and hope to better enjoy more of the same lifestyle. Instead, people are trying a whole other approach of slowing down and simplifying their lives.

The sensory overload of our generation is causing a reverse effect, and very frustrated and disillusioned people are turning to the well of simplicity. People are desperate to experience freedom from the tyranny of society's distractions and complications. They are making choices that promote a simplification of spheres of their lives.

MTV

We can see this happening in the music industry. People eventually grow tired of the typical explosions of sound, color, movement and images. Recently MTV launched *MTV Unplugged,* where artists employ performance styles that are more intimate, earthy and simple. Instead of performers standing on a stage with elaborate outfits, a full-blown sound system, explosive light show and exciting backdrops, they are instead creating a homey atmosphere with couches and chairs. They are wearing blue jeans and going acoustic with their instruments. In so doing they strike a chord of simplicity in people that releases a distinct feel of contentment and peace.

NATURE

In the midst of the craziness of busy city and suburban life, people are discovering the simple joys of nature and the outdoors. For proof, all one has to do is try to get a reservation for a campsite at any national or state park in the summer. Individuals, families and couples are finding joy in the raw simplicity of nature. Not just campgrounds but retreat centers are also a huge success because they deliver the simplicity of nature for those who are not quite willing or able to brave the challenges of the outdoors.

Quietness and solitude provide a place to reset our compass.

IN THE CHURCH

In times past, Christians found significance, meaning and purpose through their relationships with God. One's relationship with Him was the well of significance and meaning from which they drank. People experienced a fuller reality of life because they learned to develop a spiritual foundation that brought forth its consistent harvest of meaning and significance. They did not neglect the tilling of that soil.

The Scriptures clearly lay forth the principle of sowing and reaping. "A man reaps what he sows" (Gal. 6:7). The unfortunate result is that American Christianity has largely neglected the necessary tilling of the spiritual foundation of her life because she has become so content with the materialistic fruit she has been eating. Thus, the pace of life required to maintain this fruit mercilessly grinds on as the vitality of the believer's spirit all but shrivels up and dies. A healthy spirit requires doses of quietness and rest, not a continual diet of speed and clatter. As Herman Riffel says in *Learning to Hear God's Voice,* "The treasure to be found in the quiet times alone with the Lord can seldom be found in the rush of a too-busy day."[2]

THE EXTREME CHALLENGE OF AMERICAN CHRISTIANITY

Part of the problem that our society faces is that our higher standard of living provides resources and opportunities for people to seek fulfillment through physical pleasure that, in former days, were never even options. Such lifestyles can easily cause people to become numb to their need for cultivating a spiritual foundation of life. In the past physical discomfort from the harsh realities of life often drove people to seek spiritual solutions and thereby find contentment and peace. Today people are so increasingly focused on physical comfort that they have become almost oblivious to their spiritual needs and the spiritual foundation from which they need to live their lives.

American Christians live in such a society. I have often heard missionaries share how the hardest place to be a Christian today is in America. I am not referring to being a nominal or cultural Christian, but to being a believer that experiences the life Jesus and the apostles modeled for us. Such life is received only by grace and comes only when we recognize our need. We have become so confident of our abilities, opportunities and devices that we so often fail to have a faith that is desperate for God. It is hard to be desperate for God when we are content with the things of the world—not the bad, immoral things but the legitimately good things. Our enjoyment of the good has numbed us to our need for the best.

GOOD—THE ENEMY OF THE BEST

Many American Christians are so comfortable with the "good" (morally righteous and materially blessed) life that they are unwilling to pursue God with greater commitment and greater sacrifice. Other American Christians are not satisfied with their Christian lives in terms of more deeply knowing God and experiencing Him, yet they are not miserable enough to pursue Him more totally. Their blessings have served to anes-thetize them from the pain in their souls that long for deeper relationship with God. They confuse the happiness gained from their material blessing with the fullness of life gained by fully pursuing God and His kingdom. In both cases "good" has clearly become the enemy of the "best," thereby preventing people from nurturing their spiritual foundation in order that God's presence would be more fully experienced.

Even in the unsaved world people are frustrated by the inability of wealth to provide lasting and real peace and joy. There are similar rum-blings in the church. Many people are so frustrated that they are overwhelmed with a sense of holy desperation, a cry for the "real deal" of God's life in them. Such people have awakened to the reality that the truly satisfying and fulfilling life they desire cannot come by any of their own sanctified efforts or resources but only by the grace of God. Only in the place of admitted neediness does God release such a quality of life. David Trementozzi, in his book *Holy Desperation,* says: "With this desperation comes hope, because God comes to those who cry out to Him. God imparts to those who beg. God gives to those who are desperate! Once we come to the place where all of our self-confidence has been lost, it is then that we find a confidence rooted in God, not ourselves [or our things]."[3]

The bottom line is that much of the church wants to get back to basics. Many Christians are slowing their lives down and embracing simplicity because they have learned that the place of quietness is where God's voice can be heard and the impartation of His life is received.

How will this happen?

THE SABBATH PRINCIPLE

"Observe the Sabbath day by keeping it holy, as the LORD your God has commanded you. Six days you shall labor and do all your work, but the seventh day is a Sabbath to the LORD your God. On it you shall not do any work" (Deut. 5:12–14). Primary to the restoration of increased simplicity in the church will be a much greater embracing of the knowledge and experience of the Sabbath. Modern understanding of the Sabbath replaces the term with the words *vacation* or *day off.* But this is not what God meant. The Scripture says that we are to keep the Sabbath "holy." The meaning of the word *holy* in its intended Hebrew usage was "to set something apart as holy unto the Lord." We can hardly say that the common understanding of a vacation or day off is God's intention for Sabbath. The Sabbath is specifically a day that we give unto the Lord. It is a day that we set aside our own agendas, expectations and desires and instead simply give ourselves to the Lord. Today, Christian Sabbaths are not really Sabbaths because they are often the most hectic days of the week.

If a Christian would implement a true Sabbath each week, he or she would hear the voice of God more clearly and would know His presence more intimately. Such a commitment to keeping the Sabbath would be the spiritual equivalent of growing a vegetable garden or digging a well. Such investment of time reaps dividends, as does tithing. Among those living the average American lifestyle, nobody feels that they can "afford" to take a Sabbath any more than they feel they can "afford" to tithe. But such acts of faith to God always reap tremendous spiritual benefits in the lives of the disciplined ones. Such ones learn to consistently set time aside from their busy schedules. They will begin to regularly reap the life-giving fruit of their investment and living water from their wells of Sabbath discipline...for God comes to such gardens and fills such wells.

The Sabbath principle is the key for the church learning to embrace and implement the quiet place into her life. More than one day a week set aside, the Sabbath principle is in itself the foundation for a life of greater holiness and spiritual sensitivity. For at the heart of the Sabbath is the desire to come away that one might be more fully present and given to the Lord. Yes, it is a discipline, but it is also a mind-set. The Sabbath principle is a way of life for those who have realized that true Christian maturity and spirituality do not come haphazardly—they must be intentionally sought.

CHRISTIAN RETREAT CENTERS

In the church we can already see how this concept of Sabbath principle is taking root in believer's lives through the growth of Christian retreat centers.

Churches, families, couples and pastors are planning weekends and full weeks away from the normal routine of life simply for the purpose of slowing down and getting quiet before God. Such retreat centers are very conducive to quietness and rest since they are often located in the mountains or country and are away from the hustle and bustle of city life.

WORSHIP AND WAITING ON THE LORD

Indicators of movement in the church toward a fuller embracing of the quiet place can be seen in an increased emphasis on being still and quiet for periods of time in worship services. Such periods of waiting serve to be times of tremendous refreshment for those involved. In such silent stillness, physical and emotional healing is experienced, divine encouragement is received, assurance is gained. People "unplug" from the pressing anxieties and learn to simply be still and focus on Christ. Such waiting is very conducive for worship, sometimes serving as a precursor to worship and other times as a result of worship.

SPIRITUAL DISCIPLINES

Large portions of the church are realizing that authentic biblical Christianity runs contrary to not just the carnal desires of the flesh, but even the power of good intentions. Human power, talent and ability are increasingly showing themselves unable to deliver the quality of life the Bible describes as Christian. Unless believers implement specific measures of discipline and structure into their lives, their level of spiritual maturity will remain wanting. The spiritual disciplines are deliberate activities pursued in the life of the believer that provide "doorways" for grace to flow from the throne of God and into their souls. Such disciplines have often been considered commonplace in the history of the church, but to our modern understanding they somehow seem foreign or unrealistic.

Two very well-received modern classics on this subject are the books *The Spirit of the Disciplines* by Dallas Willard as well as *Celebration of Discipline* by Richard Foster. In many Bible colleges and seminaries these have become standard reading. Also, in addition to books on the spiritual disciplines, there is a great interest in the church in the multitude of daily devotional books being published. Such books are usually designed to provide a commentary or reflection on a passage of Scripture, thus helping the believer to be more disciplined and focused in his or her study and meditation of the Word.

Fasting is a discipline that continues to find many participants in the church, especially in churches where fresh outpourings of spiritual awakening have been experienced.

Those who have given themselves to the discipline of fasting likewise reap its tremendous blessings. Primary characteristics of those who fast are an ability to hear God more clearly, freedom from pressing concerns and anxieties, increased faith and divine perspective on the issues of life.

Also the discipline of extended prayer is being expressed in the church. Many believers are gathering together for what is called "the watch of the Lord." At these "watches" believers pray and worship all night long. These times are often accompanied with fasting. Believers are encouraged and motivated by such scriptures as Ezekiel 3:17, "Son of man, I have made you a watchman for the house of Israel; so hear the word I speak and give them warning from me." Christians who have given themselves to the discipline of the watch see themselves as watchmen unto the Lord that He might place His desires and concerns on their hearts for the church and the world. Such watchmen are given to praying those things forth throughout the night and early morning hours.

The quiet place, a place of intentional quiet and focused solitude, is a doorway to hearing and receiving more from the heart of the Lord. The freedom from distraction that may have been easy for David to find while tending sheep in the field must become for us a daily pursuit. As we cultivate this place, this inner sanctum, quietness will not be fearful to us; it will be a welcome release from the bombardments of outer and inner noise that seek to distract us from eternity.

May we be freed daily from subtle attachments to this world, more released that we might become better citizens and sons and daughters of our Father's kingdom.

What Now?

For group discussion:

1. Schedule a late night or all-night prayer and worship event (often called "The Watch of the Lord"). In a relaxed manner, wait on the Lord in worship and intercession.

2. In your group meeting, take twenty minutes and commit to silent, focused prayer. Discuss later how this affected you.

3. As a group, come up with a large list of all the various things in modern life that can be classified as "distraction of options." Begin to separate that which is absolutely necessary from that which is culturally imposed.

For personal application:

1. What do you think is meant by this statement: "The issue is not just about having distractions. It's about most people in our society having learned lifestyles of distractions where they lose the ability simply to be and cannot find meaning and joy apart from all toys and accruements of modern life."

2. Take an eight-hour period of time and "fast" talking. During this time think about the value of words. Ask yourself if you use words too lightly.

3. Is there an area in your life where you have regularly resigned yourself to an acceptance of the "good" and accordingly "lost your appetite" for the "best" things? How can you regain your full hunger?

A Heart
for the Poor

The church will understand we are called not just to give to the poor, but to be in relationship with the poor. Casual giving to soothe our consciences will be replaced by vital action, where our lives will intertwine with the poor, and we will see we have lessons to learn that only they can teach us.

Eagles' Wings has been leading missions teams to Honduras for the past several years. Each summer we mobilize people, finances, clothes and medical supplies and get involved in ministering throughout that wonderful country.

For the past few years, we have stayed at a hotel in the heart of Tegucigalpa, the capital city. As we began coming and going from that hotel a few years ago, I noticed a young shoeshine boy parked out in front of our hotel, who, without fail, would ask everyone in our group every time we came in or out if we needed a shoeshine.

Finally, his persistence and winsome smile won our hearts, and we spent a few minutes letting him work on our shoes. We learned that like dozens of shoeshine boys in the streets, he lived in the park. He seemed to have no parents or family to speak of. He was about ten years old.

We were amazed when we came back the next year to find Walter perched right out in front of the same hotel, ready to greet us like we had just returned from a weekend away. For the next few years, this relationship continued, and we watched him grow.

One year when we were there, one of our team members, John, noticed Walter's shoes were literally falling apart. John found some strong duct tape and fixed them temporarily until we could provide a more permanent solution.

I sat down with Walter and told him I wanted to help him. I asked him what he needed. I assumed he would ask for food or clothes. We walked to a market, and Walter took off like a shot. I stood back, expecting cookies or toys or something to be brought to the counter for me to purchase for him.

He came back a few moments later. In his hands were two cans of shoe polish and a new shoe brush and shoe rag. "With these I can shine shoes and get money!" he said, his mouth widening into a semi-toothless grin.

My eyes began to moisten, and I said, "Walter, go back and get more. Get food or whatever you need." He said no; he was fine. This was all he needed to get by.

My eyes brimming, I took Walter by the arm and grabbed two large shopping bags. We went back to the shoeshine supplies and got all I could fill in one bag. With each thrust of my arm into the sack, my anger at poverty and my frustration with my comfortable world increased. I then took the other bag and filled it with any healthy, nonperishable food item I could find and walked it to the checkout counter.

As Walter thanked me and headed back to the park, I looked around at two dozen or so other young, nameless shoeshine boys. Why had I felt such strong emotion all of a sudden? We had been working all day, distributing goods to the poor in some remote villages. I was accustomed to seeing poverty in Honduras and many other Third World nations where we had ministered. Why had this experience burst upon me with such emotion?

Then it dawned on me. I could spend hours giving clothes, medical supplies or food to a sea of faces in village after village, stepping into their makeshift huts with open sewage in the streets. I could feel a real sense of compassion and disbelief at the conditions I saw and wish that more Americans could see poverty firsthand. But what was the difference in that brief experience with Walter? What had touched me so deeply?

The difference was that, for me, Walter had a name.

Open yourself for one moment past the safety of the role of benefactor and actually allow your heart to *know* the person you are helping, and you will be ruined, because in that moment you awaken to the fact that this is a person whose daily life is the poverty that you see from your television set or give to in an offering. When you don't just give to the need, but sensitize yourself to their reality, it is a completely different thing.

A few months after my experience at the market with Walter, I watched CNN reports as a hurricane ravaged Honduras, killing thousands and literally wiping away village after village. I thought of the villages where we have ministered, thought of the shoeshine boys in the park. And then I thought of Walter, and I cried and prayed. I will be looking for him…

THE NEED IS STILL WITH US

Jesus said we would always have poor among us, and it is more true today than ever. Though the stock market continues to soar and American companies earn record profits, most of the world is sinking deeper into the quagmire of cyclical poverty.

No nation on earth has a greater net worth than the United States. But that wealth is distributed unequally. A small percentage of the wealthiest households in America own a large percentage of the nation's assets. Children comprise a high percentage of those Americans who live in poverty. Despite these glaringly apparent needs, churches across the country are minimally involved in addressing this issue. For every dollar spent on ministry to the poor, the typical church spends more than five dollars on buildings and maintenance.[1]

The need today goes beyond just giving to the poor. The church must become an agent of social change that provides workable solutions to real-life problems. Education, job training, parenting skills—all of these should not be outside the realm of the church's involvement and influence. A wonderful example of this is the Rock Church in Baltimore, pastored by Rev. Bart Pierce. This dynamic congregation has commanded the attention of their city by leading the way with drug rehabilitation programs, homes for unwed mothers and massive food distribution.

However, we make people dependent upon ourselves by mere gifts if we are not careful to accompany them with teaching and training. There is a great deal of wisdom to the proverb: Give a man a fish, and you've fed him for a meal; teach a man to fish, and you've fed him for a lifetime. To provide long-term solutions, we need to equip the underprivileged and uneducated with new skills. This requires a long-term commitment of time to teach, mentor and nurture.

Kingdom Mandates for Ministry to the Poor

The call of the kingdom to minister to the poor did not start with Jesus' teaching. God has always called those in His kingdom to be focused and faithful in ministry to the poor and oppressed. In Deuteronomy, Moses spoke to the Israelites about the mandates of living as God's people.

> There should be no poor among you, for in the land the LORD your God is giving you to possess as your inheritance, he will richly bless you, if only you fully obey the LORD your God.
>
> —DEUTERONOMY 15:4–5

In this passage Moses displays the ideal of godly society—that there should be no poor among us. He points out that our land and possessions are inherited from the Lord; therefore, it is our right to own them. But it is our right only if we fully obey the Lord our God. The promises that God makes are real, but they are also conditional upon our faithfulness to Him. It is our faithfulness and devotion to His truths, grace and love that gain us our inheritance. Moses goes on to describe some specific commands:

> Give generously to [a poor man] and do so without a grudging heart; then because of this the LORD your God will bless you in all your work and in everything you put your hand to. There will always be poor people in the land. Therefore I command you to be open-handed toward your brothers and toward the poor and needy in your land.
>
> —DEUTERONOMY 15:10–11

God does not recommend or suggest. He commands us to be open-handed toward our brothers (fellow man) and toward the poor and needy. Moses told the Israelites to give generously without a grudging heart. Moses knew the importance of the posture of our hearts when we give. To give generously to a poor man without a grudging heart is a test to see how attached we are to our possessions. Ultimately, the command to help the poor leads a man to be constantly rejoicing in the goodness and faithfulness of God.

JESUS' COMMANDS

In Christ's ministry to the poor, grace kissed truth to save the world. It is this love that we will see usher the entire world into the presence of the Lord. Jesus' heart cried out for all His brothers and sisters. The Lord's family is not complete, and we are being called as stewards to bring all those from the streets into His house. (See Matthew 22:1–14.) The table is set, and the wedding feast is waiting.

In the parable of the sheep and the goats, Jesus makes it clear that we will be judged by God if we ignore the needs of the poor but greatly rewarded if we minister to them in practical ways. (See Matthew 25:31–46.) If we minister to hungry, thirsty, lonely, sick and imprisoned people, Jesus will reward us just as if we had been doing these things for Him. To these, Jesus will say:

> Come, you who are blessed by my Father; take your inheritance, the kingdom prepared for you since the creation of the world. For I was hungry and you gave me something to eat, I was thirsty and you gave me something to drink, I was a stranger and you invited me in, I needed clothes and you clothed me, I was sick and you looked after me, I was in prison and you came to visit me.
>
> —MATTHEW 25:34–36

The Messiah made it clear that "whatever you did for one of the least of these brothers of mine, you did for me" (Matt. 25:40). Ministry to the poor is an act of worship—for as we minister to the poor, we minister to Jesus Himself.

In the parable of the Good Samaritan, Jesus told the story of a man who had been beaten, robbed and nearly killed. Left for dead, he lay on the road naked and bleeding. In this story, "a priest happened to be going down the same road, and when he saw the man, he passed by on the other side" (Luke 10:31). The most outwardly devout, religious individual passed by the poor and suffering, paying no attention.

Samaritans were an ethnic group that was looked down upon by the Jews. For a Samaritan to be right with God would probably be heresy in the eyes of most Jews in Jesus' day. And yet Jesus said the Samaritan was the only one who truly fulfilled the law of love.

> But a Samaritan, as he traveled, came where the man was; and when he saw him, he took pity on him. He went to him and bandaged his wounds, pouring on oil and wine. Then he put the man on his own donkey, took him to an inn and took care of him. The next day he took out two silver coins and gave them to the innkeeper. "Look after him," he said, "and when I return, I will reimburse you for any extra expense you may have."
>
> —Luke 10:33–35

The priest in this story, though his highest calling was ministry unto God, failed to see how ministry to others *was* ministry to God. Likewise, if we fail to love others and live that which we preach, we have gained nothing. God is raising up a generation that places a higher value on ministry to and interaction with the poor and broken. This generation will know the Isaiah 61 favor of God upon them as they reach out to touch the broken.

GOD'S JUDGMENTS

God has no tolerance for the wealthy who refuse to share their resources with others.

Now this was the sin of your sister Sodom: She and her daughters were arrogant, overfed and unconcerned; they did not help the poor and needy. They were haughty and did detestable things before me. Therefore I did away with them as you have seen.

—EZEKIEL 16:49–50

The sin pointed out in Sodom was not the only perversion we normally associate with that city. Here, the prophet gives a fuller depiction of the debauchery of the town and shows that the judgment of God came on them not only for their "detestable" actions, but also for their arrogance and hardness of heart, which manifested itself in indifference to the plight of the poor.

God places little value on religious practice that does not minister to the poor and hurting in practical ways. James said:

If anyone considers himself religious and yet does not keep a tight rein on his tongue, he deceives himself and his religion is worthless. Religion that God our Father accepts as pure and faultless is this: to look after orphans and widows in their distress and to keep oneself from being polluted by the world.

—JAMES 1:26–27

LETTING OUR LIGHT SHINE

You are the light of the world. A city on a hill cannot be hidden. Neither do people light a lamp and put it under a bowl. Instead they put it on its stand, and it gives light to everyone in the house. In the same way, let your light shine before men, that they may see your good deeds and praise your Father in heaven.

—MATTHEW 5:14–16

When a local expression of the body of Christ does not reach out to their community, the effectiveness of their witness is sadly lost. Unless we actively minister to the lost, the poor and the hurting, we will be hiding our lamp under a bowl. If we desire to be light to the world, then we must allow good deeds to be seen. There are no scriptures in the New Testament instructing believers to keep their expression of faith in a church building. In fact, the Bible calls us to do the opposite! Jesus said, "Go to the street corners..." (Matt. 22:9). The temple we are called to build is not a natural one any longer, but a spiritual one, made of "living stones" (1 Pet. 2:5). There are some wonderful ministries setting excellent examples for the rest of the body in doing just that.

Blood 'N Fire, an inner-city ministry based in Atlanta, Georgia, is a great example of a church impacting the community around them. This wellspring of hope feeds the homeless every day, shelters many and pursues ongoing relationships while ministering in the inner-city projects of Atlanta. The mission of Blood 'N Fire, according to David VanCronkite, founder and leader, is to empower the poor to rebuild the cities of the nations....Give them Jesus, disciple and train them and then turn them loose to plant churches and rebuild cities.

An important part of Blood 'N Fire's ministry is serving a meal as part of their Sunday church service. The fellowship in having a meal together is something Jesus emphasized throughout His time on earth. There is a tremendous amount of love and care exchanged while sharing a meal with someone. Jesus did not give the twelve disciples going-away presents. He joined them in the Last Supper. It is important to recognize that we need to bring the poor, sick and lost into our lives instead of isolating them along with their problems.

Blood 'N Fire is ministering in the midst of radical poverty, violence and degradation, with rampant unemployment and under-employment. Street life is radical with drugs, gangs and poverty. In that setting, an extreme approach is necessary: extreme worship, extreme commitment, an extreme Jesus.

Bart Campolo is another radical who is calling the church not to service to the poor, but relationship with the poor. His program, MissionYear, takes young people and places them in small teams in local, urban churches for one year. The context of the inner city is in some ways a totally foreign culture to these young people.

For a year they live and serve as members of these local churches, learning firsthand what it is like to live on the "other side." This relationship focus produces a lasting impact that will shape these young people and the way they relate to the inner city and its people for the rest of their lives.

PUTTING FAITH INTO ACTION

God is raising up a generation who will be doers of the Word, not just hearers. (See James 1:22.) The day has arrived where congregations will be changed in thought and then implement in action the Word they hear preached on Sunday morning. This generation will allow the Word of the Lord to burn in them, gripping their hearts, changing their lives and ultimately, making them vessels of God's love and compassion for the poor, the lost and the hurting.

Giving to the poor is a spiritual discipline, just as powerful as prayer and fasting. In the Sermon on the Mount, Jesus taught about giving to the needy before He addressed the subjects of prayer and fasting. (See Matthew 6:1–18.)

One of the most important factors in the growth of the New Testament believers was their care for each other and for the widows and orphans in their midst. After the power of the Holy Spirit fell upon the believers in the upper room and three thousand were saved, the Christians did not just return to their homes and go back to "business as usual." They formed a community where every need was met and every person was cared for.

> All the believers were one in heart and mind. No one claimed that any of his possessions were his own, but they shared everything they had. With great power the apostles continued to testify to the resurrection of the Lord Jesus, and much grace was upon them all. There were no needy persons among them. For from time to time those who owned lands or houses sold them, brought the money from the sales and put it at the apostles' feet, and it was distributed to anyone as he had need.
>
> —ACTS 4:32–35

Imagine a church in your city where members regularly, intentionally simplified their lifestyles in order to give extravagant offerings to the poor. Imagine a church where everyone was of "one heart and mind," giving freely of their possessions, recognizing stewardship rather than striving for ownership. Could it be that one of the keys to the radical signs and wonders regularly seen by the New Testament church was their lack of attachment to earthly things?

While Protestantism has deposited in Christians a rich understanding of salvation by grace, there is much we need to learn from the historic churches who showed their salvation with their works. One of the greatest strengths of the Catholic church is that they give men and women an opportunity to live a life of simplicity before God, giving up worldly wealth and riches in pursuit of a life of ministry unto God and others. We can gain much wisdom from the simplicity and selflessness of these lives of service. Let us strive to lead lives of greater simplicity and compassion, rejecting the world's distractions in pursuit of the Father's will.

A CALL TO SIMPLICITY

George Mueller's life is a testimony of simplicity before God, illuminating God's desire to be the sole provider of all we need and desire. Mueller spent much of his life establishing orphan houses for thousands of English children. He never asked anyone for support or let people know of his needs, but his needs were always sovereignly met by the provision of God. One biographer commented: "Because he knew his Father was so rich, benevolent, and forgiving, he was free to ask for and obtain great blessings."[2]

Not only did Mueller fulfill his calling by housing thousands of orphans, but his faith and trust in the Lord has provided millions of people with inspiration and motivation. Mueller's life is an illustration of the blessings inherited when we pursue the Father's heart for the poor. The physical blessings such as housing, food, medical and educational supplies and furniture are part of the provision. But the eternal blessings of faith, humility, love and wisdom are the crown of Mueller's outreach to the poor. Mueller wrote of one situation:

Patience and faith are still needed. My desire is to let patience have its perfect work. Not one penny has come in today for the building fund, but five more orphans have applied for admission. The more I look at things according to natural appearances, the less likely it seems that I will ever get the sum I need. But I have faith in God, and my expectation is from Him alone. The Lord can change the circumstances instantly. I continue, therefore, to wait upon God and seek to encourage my heart by His Word. While He delays giving me answers, I will be occupied in His blessed work.[3]

Mueller's simple dependence and contentment in God is what produced wisdom, revelation and blessings throughout his ministry to the poor. Seeking God's heart made George Mueller a man who was abandoned to reaching the poor, while knowing God's heart made him a man who has touched millions of lives.

An American earning even a most basic wage maintains a standard of living vastly higher than most of the rest of the world. We are simply unaware of the enormous abundance in which we live—and the enormous need in the nations. May the Lord continue to speak to His body in the prosperous West about having a heart of compassion for the poor of our own country and of the world. He is still dwelling with the least of these—and waiting for us to meet Him there.

What Now?

For group discussion:

1. What does your church currently do to give to the poor in your specific geographic area (not including foreign missions giving)? How can that grow?

2. Decide to take a Sunday or Wednesday night and do the works of Jesus. Have your group gather food, blankets and other essentials and minister life and prayer to the poor in your area.

3. In the parable, the master tells his servants to go into the streets and invite them to the wedding feast. Would you consider having a "wedding feast" for the poor in your area, teaching on our relationship with God?

For personal application:

1. Whom do you personally know as a friend who is poor? How can you help that person grow in all areas of life?

2. Consider going on a fast and setting aside the money you would have spent on food to give to the poor.

3. Drive through a poor neighborhood one day and later on, write down your thoughts and turn them into prayers.

11

⁓

Restoring the Tabernacle of David

The next generation will be abandoned in worship. Cultural restrictions on worship will fall, replaced by a biblical understanding of the experience and power of worship.

I took a group of worshipers and intercessors to a large park in Tel Aviv overlooking the Mediterranean. As it was a holiday, the area was flooded with hundreds of families having picnics and teenagers just "hanging out."

We sat down as a group and began to worship. We really felt the presence of the Lord in a strong way, and one of the ladies in our group who had brought several praise flags with her took one out and began waving it to the Lord.

It is hard to explain what happened next. It was one of those "you had to be there" experiences. Suddenly, we were gripped with a tremendous sense of freedom and began walking all over the park, singing, waving flags and blowing shofars.

We happened upon a group of about twenty-five teenage boys who were beating bongo drums. We walked up to them and started teaching them a simple praise song. They began to sing and play along. Within minutes, there were literally scores of people drawn to the flags and the drum beats. They began to sing, clap their hands, lift their hands and dance. The Israelis brought out their cameras, and two of them their video cameras, recording this event. There was extraordinary openness to the simplicity of joy expressed in music.

I have heard a lot about worship evangelism and the song of the Lord "going to the streets," but this was by far the most incredible foretaste I have ever experienced.

The Spirit of freedom is invading our comfort zones. He is bringing new sounds, new dances and taking us to new places in worship. We are going to higher heights and deeper depths in God. He is drawing us into the holy flame of divine fire. We are no longer satisfied with an outer court experience. The bride is ravished with longing and desire for her bridegroom, and nothing can satisfy us except the passionate release that comes from wholehearted intimacy with Him. The Spirit and the bride say, "Come!" (See Revelation 22:17.)

EXPERIENCING GOD

We will enter into hours and days of extended waiting in His presence. We will hear His heartbeat and know His voice. We will be overcome with one relentless, insatiable craving—more of Him. Past the outer courts of our own need, worship will be all about ministering to the Lord Himself. A holy company of End-Time Levites will be brought forth in the nations of the earth to tend to the flame of the Lord, seeing that it does not burn out day or night. Jealousy for His house will consume us, and once again His house will be called a house of prayer for all nations. Religious machinations will cease as we are undone by His glory and His love. An hour in His presence, gazing into His eyes of beauty, will accomplish more than weeks of counseling and human effort at healing our souls. We will understand that the Healer *is* healing, and simply being with Him cleanses, refreshes and satisfies.

RELEASING THE HEART OF MARY

Passion for His presence will mark all that we are, and nothing will be more important than maintaining His presence in our midst. Human striving and political ambition will fade into irrelevance. The King is here. There is no need for earthly wisdom. Wisdom Himself is here, speaking into our hearts.

The heart of Mary will be released, and we will sit at His feet and know the penetrating gaze of His blazing eyes. Consuming us, He will be our all in all. The alabaster box of our lives will be gladly broken, and the fragrant oil of our lives, wasted on Him, will fill the air. Presence will be valued over service. Brokenness over productivity. Intimacy over conquest. (See John 12:1–11.)

Ancient songs, ancient sounds, will be lifted as ancient prayers to the Ancient of Days. And He will rise and destroy ancient strongholds. (See Daniel 7:9.)

WORSHIP IS A PLACE

For too long we have thought of worship as an activity. We have worship services scheduled at 11:00 A.M. Sunday morning all across the country. Worship teams, worship recordings and worship conferences all cause us to think of worship as an activity mainly marked by singing, clapping and perhaps dancing. While this is certainly part of worship, it is only a part. Our minds are being broadened to understand more fully the source, impact and scope of true worship.

THE THRONE ROOM

The throne room of God is described by John:

> At once I was in the Spirit, and there before me was a throne in heaven with someone sitting on it. And the one who sat there had the appearance of jasper and carnelian. A rainbow, resembling an emerald, encircled the throne. *Surrounding the throne were twenty-four other thrones, and seated on them were twenty-four elders.* They were dressed in white and had crowns of gold on their heads. From the throne came *flashes of lightning, rumblings*

and *peals of thunder.* Before the throne, *seven lamps were blazing.* These are the seven spirits of God. Also before the throne there was what looked like a sea of glass, clear as crystal.

In the center, around the throne, were four living creatures, and they were covered with eyes, in front and in back. The first living creature was like a lion, the second was like an ox, the third had a face like a man, the fourth was like a flying eagle. Each of the four living creatures had six wings and was covered with eyes all around, even under his wings. Day and night they never stop saying: "Holy, holy, holy is the Lord God Almighty, who was, and is, and is to come."

Whenever the living creatures give glory, honor and thanks to him who sits on the throne and who lives for ever and ever, the twenty-four elders fall down before him who sits on the throne, and worship him who lives for ever and ever. They lay their crowns before the throne and say: "You are worthy, our Lord and God, to receive glory and honor and power, for you created all things, and by your will they were created and have their being."

—REVELATION 4:2–11, EMPHASIS ADDED

Take some time right now, before you read any farther, and meditate on this passage. As you read it, picture this scene in your mind.

There is a real throne room. This is a real place. It is the seat of universal government. The uncreated God, the Ancient of Days, sits enthroned in glory and splendor. This is not a metaphor or a word picture. It is literally the throne room of the King, who is our Father.

The throne room is more dramatic and impacting and fantastic than anything Hollywood could ever create. Lightning, thunder, fire, the twenty-four elders, the four creatures—no special effects could come close to the literal awesomeness of this place. And above all sits the focus of all adoration—God Almighty.

When Isaiah was granted a sensory encounter with this place, he fell upon his face in utter terror, aware that he could not live in this atmosphere of sheer and absolute holiness.

> In the year that King Uzziah died, I saw the Lord seated on a throne, high and exalted, and the train of his robe filled the temple. Above him were seraphs, each with six wings: With two wings they covered their faces, with two they covered their feet, and with two they were flying. And they were calling to one another: "Holy, holy, holy is the LORD Almighty; the whole earth is full of his glory." At the sound of their voices the doorposts and thresholds shook and the temple was filled with smoke. "Woe to me!" I cried. "I am ruined! For I am a man of unclean lips, and I live among a people of unclean lips, and my eyes have seen the King, the LORD Almighty."
>
> —ISAIAH 6:1–5

The seraph quickly came to Isaiah's assistance, cleansing him with a live coal from the altar, lest he perish. Likewise, we cannot see God's throne room, let alone have access to it, without the application of divine atonement. We have no access to the Father in our sinful state.

If we look again at the scene in the throne room, we will see how God provided access for us.

> Then I saw a Lamb, looking as if it had been slain, standing in the center of the throne, encircled by the four living creatures and the elders. He had seven horns and seven eyes, which are the seven spirits of God sent out into all the earth. He came and took the scroll from the right hand of him who sat on the throne. And when he had taken it, the four living creatures and the twenty-four elders fell down before the Lamb. Each one had a harp and they were holding golden bowls full of incense, which are the prayers of the saints. And they sang a new song:
>
> "You are worthy to take the scroll and to open its seals, because you were slain, and with your blood you purchased men for God from every tribe and language and people and nation. You have made them to be a kingdom and priests to serve our God, and they will reign on the earth." Then I looked and heard the voice of many angels, numbering thousands upon thousands, and ten thousand

times ten thousand. They encircled the throne and the living creatures and the elders. In a loud voice they sang: "Worthy is the Lamb, who was slain, to receive power and wealth and wisdom and strength and honor and glory and praise!" Then I heard every creature in heaven and on earth and under the earth and on the sea, and all that is in them, singing: "To him who sits on the throne and to the Lamb be praise and honor and glory and power, for ever and ever!" The four living creatures said, "Amen," and the elders fell down and worshiped.

—Revelation 5:6–14

Alone and separated from God by the guilt of our sin, we look up, and we see the Lion, who is a Lamb. He has paid the price! The blood of mercy flows on the altar. The purest substance in the created order erases Adam's stain from our souls. We have fellowship with God, for we are now part of His family. From this place of release and cleansing, this place of utter freedom and joy, we become aware of the thunderous sights and sounds that are everywhere in this place. And we realize that the very atmosphere of heaven, our home, is music! Not just music—but Music. The original Song! The stars sing as they did at Creation—the mountains and the hills cry out—the trees of the field clap their hands! (See Isaiah 55:12.)

These tones and sounds and colors swirl around Him, and suddenly we become aware that we are pulsating with this Song. We are not "singing," as we would know it here on earth. Rather, our entire being literally *becomes* part of the song! We *are* a sound, a note, a tone—and the sound of grace—the song He has been singing over us all our lives—wells up from every part of us and joins this symphony of praise.

Now

The above verses describing the worship of the Lamb do not talk about something that is *going* to happen, future tense, as we usually think of it. They are describing something that *already* has occurred. He is the Lamb who was "slain from the foundation of the world" (Rev. 13:8, NKJV). Outside of time, the Lamb has been already been crowned. Worship emanates from the timeless place of the eternal God who has already accomplished His plan in Christ. We are waiting for His kingdom to come here, in time and space. But outside of this mortal realm, we are already seated in heavenly places in Christ, rejoicing with the elders, creatures and angels at all that has been wrought through the obedience of Christ.

This throne room revelation will become the beginning place for worship in this hour. As we gather in physical buildings here in time and space, we will understand that in the most real way we are joining the activity of heaven. We are joining the angels, the elders and the cloud of witnesses. Even though we see through this glass darkly, still, we realize we are entering an eternal realm in our worship. We are participating in throne room activity. The chorus of worship and intercession lifted up around the planet joins and is mixed with that which is present in the halls of heaven. Time and eternity meet. Heaven and earth mingle. The "now" and the "not yet" are wed in this place.

THE SOUNDS OF HEAVEN—
BIBLICAL WORSHIP VS. CULTURAL

If you could physically hear the worship going on in heaven at this moment, what do you think it would sound like? What do you think the angels' voices sound like? What about the creatures? How would those sounds mix with the background of the thunder, lightening, fire and smoke?

Chances are, the sounds of heavenly worship are far different than our typical Sunday morning song service. We might even be scared at some of the sounds of heaven. They might sound intense, blinding, overwhelming.

Worship is one aspect of our walk with the Lord that has been given a clear blueprint in Scripture. This blueprint manifests through the particular culture in which we live. However, where man's culture and God's blueprint clash, our culture must yield. God has been very clear and specific about the kind of sacrifice He looks for in our worship.

Here are some examples of biblical worship:

- Standing—2 Chronicles 9:7
- Lifting our hands—Psalm 28:2, 1 Timothy 2:8
- Clapping our hands—Psalm 47:1
- Bowing—Psalm 95:6
- With all forms of musical instruments—Psalm 150
- Loudly, with crashing symbols—Psalm 150
- Dancing—Exodus 15:20; Psalm 30:11
- Leaping—Acts 3:8
- Shouting—Psalm 47:1

In the past, we have been stifled in the expression of our worship because we have allowed our culture to dictate to us what is appropriate. That is changing. God is raising up a radical generation of passionate worshipers who will fully release worship to God with all their heart, all their soul and all their might.

DANCE, CHILDREN, DANCE

Specifically, I believe the American church has been captive in disobedience to the Lord in regard to worshiping Him in dance. Our American culture is one of the few cultures on the planet that does not have a strong tradition of folk dance. Most other cultures have traditional dances as a part of their way of life. They view folk dancing as a wholesome activity that helps celebrate and strengthen the bond between family and friends. In America, dancing is almost totally associated with nightclubs and has strong sexual connotations. This cultural entrapment has kept the church from being released into the power and anointing that comes from abandoning oneself before the Lord in dance.

I have never been able to understand the thinking of many churches that would discourage or even not allow people to dance before the Lord in a worship service. These same churches send their teenagers to Christian music festivals or contemporary Christian music concerts. There, the leaders hope the teens will like the groups enough that they will be satisfied with Christian rock, the alternative to secular music. The very same churches that would not allow dancing, shouting and loud exclamations in their worship service now *hope* that their young people do these things at a Christian rock concert. It is deemed appropriate there.

What kind of faulty logic is this? What more appropriate place could there be to give oneself totally to the Lord—spirit, soul and body—than in worship! Is our God not worthy of this extravagant an offering? Should it be encouraged for this kind of release to be offered in the soulish context of *entertainment* but disallowed in God-centered worship?

Many people use the excuse that they don't need to worship the Lord in the scriptural, demonstrative ways He has ordained because they are worshiping Him "in their hearts, in their own way." However, it is not enough to simply say that we are worshiping God "in our hearts." He commands that we worship Him outwardly, in the midst of the congregation. It is not enough to say we are worshiping God "in our own way." He doesn't want your way. He wants His way.

Our church cultures have had a worship "comfort zone"—an acceptable look and sound for worship. God is about to blast us completely out of our comfort zone. Do you remember Isaiah's vision? There is nothing comfortable about being in God's presence. Ecstatic, exuberant, overwhelming, stripping, intense, intimate, rushing, incomprehensible, fabulous, terrifying, supernatural—yes. Ordinary? No.

I heard a comment for years in reference to dancing in worship: "It doesn't matter how high you jump. It matters how straight you walk when you come down." This statement, and the attitude it conveys, is often used to support a mind-set that says it doesn't really matter if you worship outwardly and demonstratively or not, as long as your "heart is right." This is simply not true. Part of our obedience, part of our heart being right, is following the scriptural mandates of worship.

Obviously, all the singing, shouting, dancing and clapping we do is vain and empty if our hearts are hard and our spirits polluted. The Scripture is clear that the Lord is looking for the sacrifice of a broken and contrite heart. Shouting, clapping and dancing can easily become another form of religious bondage. Any action devoid of a sincere and consistently tender-ized heart is already headed down the road to meaningless, powerless, religious exercise.

But if we are not worshiping the Lord in outward, demonstrative, bibli-cally prescribed ways, could it be that it is a result of our sin or unresolved pain? Do we *refuse* to dance because we will look foolish? That could be evidence of pride. Are we *afraid* to dance because of what others might think? That could be evidence of fear of man. God wants us *free.* And while dancing in worship is certainly not a guarantee of inner freedom, there is deliverance and release that comes when we give our inhibitions and fears to God and worship Him in this way.

Am I saying that all people, everywhere, must always be involved in every one of the scriptural worship styles mentioned above? Must everyone dance, or shout, or clap in every worship service? Of course not. Certainly, the Lord is not looking for robots or cheerleaders who do all the same things at the same time. Worship is an intensely individual experience; we express ourselves to the Lord with the verbal and physical vocabulary we feel would please Him at that moment.

I am saying that when individuals or congregations have rarely or never moved in each of the forms of worship, that it is often a sign of a need for release. In other words, people who have *never* lifted their hands or *never* danced in worship often need to overcome whatever is stopping them and respond to the Lord in this way.

WHAT ABOUT EMOTIONALISM?

When I speak on this topic in churches and seminars, I am often asked, "How do we keep from getting into emotionalism?"

My response is twofold. First, I would remind us that we serve a highly emotional God, and we have been created in His image. A whole host of emotions are ascribed to God in the Scriptures. He is seen laughing, rejoicing and singing. He is seen as full of wrath, jealous and full of delight. A look at Jesus' life shows Him fully experiencing the range of human emotions.

Secondly, I would suggest that emotionalism is being ruled, or controlled, by our emotions. Emotionalism is not about the level of freedom for release or expression of our emotions. Rather, it relates to the level of rulership that emotions have in our lives. Thus, an individual who rarely expresses emotions may actually be ruled by emotionalism.

Hyping individuals or crowds into an emotional state for the purpose of controlling them is dangerous emotionalism. Leading people into abandoned worship where they fully release their hearts and lives in the presence of the living God is a very different thing. There is no more appropriate place for the full expression of joy, laughter, righteous anger, holy jealousy, deep repentance, yearning, victory and love than the throne room.

Our lives are to be ruled by Christ through the power of the Holy Spirit and the influence of the Word of God, as we daily understand that this world is not our home. We are seated "in heavenly places in Christ" (Eph. 2:6, KJV). So because we are dead to this world and the things in it, we can be fully released into life and life abundantly. Can you imagine "life abundantly" without the full expression of emotion (John 10:10)? Can you imagine any more appropriate place for the expression of emotions than to the God who created you with them?

On a corporate level, this generation is going to regularly encourage the people of God toward full release and expression of all the forms called for by the Lord in biblical worship. They are going to be released from the constraints of what looks and sounds right in our culture and draw water from the ancient well of biblical worship. This will be vitally necessary, because worship is not about us or our comfort zone. There is never anything ordinary about being in the throne room in the presence of God. C. S. Lewis, in speaking of Aslan the Lion—his picture of God—wrote, "He is not a tame lion...He isn't safe, but He is Good."[1]

THE HARP AND THE BOWL

And when he had taken it, the four living creatures and the twenty-four elders fell down before the Lamb. Each one had a harp and they were holding golden bowls full of incense, which are the prayers of the saints.

—REVELATION 5:8

This passage contains a key for the people of God. The setting is the throne room. The leaders are the twenty-four elders. Each one has a harp. What does a harp represent? Music, of course. And each has a bowl of incense, representing prayer. The harp and the bowl together are lifted before the Lord as they worship. I believe there are several important lessons to be drawn from this passage.

We all want our prayers to be effective, but all too often we are praying from an earthly perspective. We must pray from the perspective of the throne room. What is the difference?

Earth-centered prayers are reactions to circumstances. We feel overcome by life, or we are challenged by a crisis, perhaps personal, perhaps in your church, or even a global problem. We cry out. But our attention and focus is not on the Lord. It is on the situation. While God, in His mercy, certainly hears these prayers, we often are not comforted much by them. We spend several minutes rehearsing our problem or situation, focused on the trauma we are facing and growing more anxious by the minute. We may get very excited, especially if the situation is a crucial one, and shout or pace in prayer, desperate for a breakthrough.

In contrast, a throne room-centered prayer begins with an experiential understanding that God is in heaven, ruling over this circumstance. No matter how desperate the situation may seem, He is working all things, including this, together for our good because we love Him, and He loves us. (See Romans 8:28.) Granted, sometimes it is not easy to get to a living realization of this, especially when the enemy throws miserable fiery arrows at us to discourage and overwhelm us. But we must battle through our emotions until we lay hold of the peace that passes all understanding that comes only from being in His presence.

From that place, we may indeed be led into very loud and exciting prayers as we participate in spiritual warfare over the situation and pour out the petition of our very souls to the Lord. But the starting place is a place of peace and unshakeable confidence in the reality of the goodness of God. The focus of the prayer is not on a predetermined answer that we are demanding. Rather, we are laboring for the birthing of God's purpose, aware that His thoughts and ways are higher than our own. We are standing on the Word, not just our interpretation of it.

Worship is required from all living creatures.

I find it so interesting that the passage in Revelation 5:8 describes each of the twenty-four elders holding a harp and a bowl. Imagine, with the entire heavenly host crying out and creating music, that these esteemed elders still are engaged in worship and intercession.

Worship and intercession in the throne room is the place of the release of the human heart to God. It is the context in which we bare our souls to a loving, faithful Father. We become our most real selves there because no pretense is needed. Our natural minds and flesh resist this place, this process, because inherently we realize it requires honesty, vulnerability and change. We cannot be in His presence, really, without being changed. And in our fallenness we resist change and vulnerability. We would rather quickly cover our nakedness with a fig leaf of distraction or even religious good works, rather than being broken by the unbearable voice of love.

You need to see that it is *your* voice God is waiting to hear. It is *your* breath from your lungs that He is waiting to be released to Him. It is *your* song He is waiting to hear sung. The worship team cannot "do" your worship for you! The intercessors cannot pray your heart for you! You were created *for His pleasure!* He is delighted when you delight in Him. He is an intensely personal God and has an individual calling and relationship with every person. Worship and intercession are not spectator events that we let "professionals" do. Rather, they are the greatest privilege of the redeemed and the requirement of all creation.

> Let everything that has breath praise the LORD. Praise the LORD.
> —PSALM 150:6

Finally, I believe this generation is about to experience the raising up of the house of the Lord, which is to be called a house of prayer for all people. In cities all around the world, praying worshipers are finding one another across denominational and racial boundaries, and they are crying out to God for a genuine grace of His presence to manifest in their city. This is leading to a call for centers of prayer and worship, where God's people throughout a region can gather day and night for literal twenty-four hour worship and intercession. Some of these centers will be in local churches; some will be in homes; some will be in neutral sites—buildings that have no connection to any one local church but become a meeting place for the church of the city.

As this blanket of worship and prayer rises like incense before the Lord, His Spirit will brood over the city and continually birth and nurture His purposes. Through the coming together of apostolic leaders, the unified regions will join with other regions like links in a chain, strengthening the presence of the kingdom.

God will hear the cries of His people. When His people turn to Him with all their hearts, forsaking all their sinful ways, and refuse to rely on the arm of flesh to attempt to accomplish eternal purposes, He will bare His holy arm and release His zeal. His people will be truly convinced that it is not by might or power, but only through His Spirit. (See Zechariah 4:6.) We will be willing to believe Him for radical transformation in their lives. We will then understand that our primary directions of ministry are *upward* to the Lord and *outward* to the lost. The self-centered focus we have had for so long will fade because our needs will be met by simply dwelling in His presence and gazing on Him.

As we see Him, worship is released and rises to Him. As we worship Him, He releases more of His glory. As we experience more of His glory, deeper worship is released from our hearts to Him. As more worship rises to Him, He releases greater revelations of His glory, and this causes us to worship Him more passionately. As we do, His inexpressible love opens more to us and we taste more of His goodness. As we do, our hearts long to pour back to Him all that we are, and we worship Him with our very breath. And so the divine dance of worship continues, the Bridegroom leading the bride deeper and deeper into the chambers of His heart.

What Now?

For group discussion:

1. Talk about the first time you lifted your hands to the Lord, or other firsts in worship. What helped free you to be more abandoned in worship?

2. Discuss ways in worship that you would like to see your group or church grow. Pray for the release of this form of expression, and look for how it glorifies the Messiah.

3. Take some time to consider the throne of God as described in Revelation 4 and 5. Describe how you think the music might sound. What might it look like there? See the scene John describes with the eyes of your heart.

For personal application:

1. What is an area of worship you desire to move in, but have not done so yet? Consider what is holding you back from freedom in that expression. What does it feel like when you are released to worship the Lord in a free and uninhibited way?

2. How do you react when you are distracted by others' worship if it is loud or demonstrative? What might that say about the fruit of the Spirit in your life?

3. Put on an instrumental worship tape and make up a song to sing to the Lord. If you have trouble getting started, use one of the psalms as a starting place.

12

Israel

The church will understand more fully the uniqueness of Israel in the plans and purposes of the Lord and rediscover the Jewish roots of our faith.

It was late at night and I was walking home from a birthday party, headed to my apartment in Jerusalem. Suddenly I heard the sound of loud, live music filling the streets. I followed the sound, and as I approached the center of town, I realized it was coming from the court-yard of the Great Synagogue. This synagogue contains the offices of the chief rabbinate.

I drew near to the square in front of the synagogue and saw literally hundreds of young Jewish people dancing, singing and clapping their hands with exuberance. The young men and young ladies were dancing separately, with a divider in the center. The band was playing enthusiastically, and if one did not know differently, it seemed like a high-powered worship service at a fiery, charismatic church.

I walked up to the side and overheard a very well-dressed young man who looked about twenty years old speaking English. I asked him where he was from, and he told me he was from Boston. I asked him to tell me what he was doing in Israel and what this celebration was all about.

He told me he was the son of a successful lawyer and had come to study in *yeshiva,* a school of religious training for young people, for one year. He was not sure what he wanted to do with his life, but he was strongly considering becoming a rabbi.

At this point I overheard the musicians singing a song with great gusto. "Messiah, Messiah!" they sang in Hebrew.

Interested in engaging the young man in deeper conversation, I asked him what a Messiah was. From there we launched into an intense discussion as he joyfully explained to me that the Messiah was the King of Israel who one day would come to rule all the nations. He would bring goodness and peace to the earth, and all evil would fall away under His domain.

I asked him how we would know when Messiah would come, and he explained to me that before the Messiah would come, Elijah the prophet would return and help prepare Israel for Messiah's coming. (See Malachi 4:5.) He then explained to me with great fervor how at that time, a great *shofar* (a ram's horn trumpet) would be blown, and miraculously, all over the world Jewish people would hear the sound of this trumpet and immediately return to Israel.

I was so impressed with this young man—his fervor, his zeal. Well-dressed and well-spoken, he understood what he was telling me was supernatural, but he obviously believed it wholeheartedly.

I then asked him how all the Jewish people from around the world were going to miraculously be transported back to Jerusalem when Elijah came. He said, "Well, we really don't know what it means, but the prophet says they will come on eagles' wings."

We finished our conversation, and I smiled deeply as I walked away.

UNIQUE IN THE EARTH

The past and present of the story of Israel is like the story of no other nation or people group. The divine drama that is unfolding through the centuries as the purposes of God have been and are being seen through these children of Abraham are amazing. To begin with, we see that the

Jewish people were born through a man who may have been the most influential man ever to walk the planet.

THE FATHER OF US ALL

> The LORD had said to Abram, "Leave your country, your people and your father's household and go to the land I will show you. I will make you into a great nation and I will bless you; I will make your name great, and you will be a blessing. I will bless those who bless you, and whoever curses you I will curse; and all peoples on earth will be blessed through you." So Abram left, as the LORD had told him.
>
> —GENESIS 12:1–4

Consider for a moment the billions of people throughout history—Jewish, Christian and Muslim—who all consider this man Abraham to be their father. Abraham lived in the midst of an idolatrous culture where polytheism was the norm. Most scholars believe that the people in his area during this time worshiped the moon and stars. Yet above the din of this idolatrous atmosphere, Abraham heard one voice speaking more deeply, more clearly, to his heart. Without ever having seen or known the concept that there could be one real, personal God, Abram responded to the voice of the Lord. In so doing, monotheism as a concept was birthed into the earth, and righteousness leading to faith was birthed in his heart. He secured for himself an everlasting lineage of all those who live by faith and call on the name of the Lord.

> We have been saying that Abraham's faith was credited to him as righteousness. Under what circumstances was it credited? Was it after he was circumcised, or before? It was not after, but before! And he received the sign of circumcision, a seal of the righteousness that he had by faith while he was still uncircumcised. So then, he is the father of all who believe but have not been circumcised, in order that righteousness might be credited to them. And he is also the father of the circumcised who not only are circumcised but who

also walk in the footsteps of the faith that our father Abraham had before he was circumcised.

It was not through law that Abraham and his offspring received the promise that he would be heir of the world, but through the righteousness that comes by faith. For if those who live by law are heirs, faith has no value and the promise is worthless, because law brings wrath. And where there is no law there is no transgression.

Therefore, the promise comes by faith, so that it may be by grace and may be guaranteed to all Abraham's offspring—not only to those who are of the law but also to those who are of the faith of Abraham. He is the father of us all.

—ROMANS 4:9–16

Imagine the faith necessary to believe that you have discovered the truth when there is no precedent or context in which to find support! *Abraham literally determined the course of human history by hearing, believing and responding to the voice of the Lord.* Let us believe that the people of God today will rediscover the example of Abraham. Hearing, believing and responding is the process whereby we also can shape history.

THE LAND

Many Christians are awakening to the fact that the Lord is not returning to Tokyo, New York or London. He will set His feet and His throne upon a literal physical city—the city of Jerusalem.

Consider the cry of the psalmist, which should command our hearts today. "Pray for the peace of Jerusalem: they shall prosper that love thee" (Ps. 122:6, KJV). New York may be the capital city of the kingdoms of this world, but Jerusalem is the capital city of the universe. It is the geographic center of the unfolding of the purposes of the Lord, where eventually His glory will be seen once again. The ark of His *shekinah* presence rested there once, and it will rest there again!

Israel, this tiny nation, lies at the heart of the earth, nestled between the three continents of Asia, Africa and Europe. In ancient times, it was the thoroughfare for trade that would come in from the Mediterranean and then go out to Babylon, Damascus and Asia. This is the land of Moses and Joshua, of David and Solomon. Jesus walked in this land, taught His disciples and sent them out to change the world. Everything about the land—its climate, geography, wildlife—all these factors played an influence on the people of the Bible as God spoke to them and made Himself real to them here.

SCATTERED

There are many things that make the generation you and I live in unique in human history. Examples include the population explosion, technology and the terror of new, seemingly unstoppable diseases. Many factors point to the fact that the era in which we have been born is unprecedented in human history.

However, for students of the Word, there is one sign above all others that shouts out to us, and that is the sign of Israel.

No other nation in human history has survived not just one, but two devastating scatterings and then been regathered and reestablished in her ancient boundaries. The first exile, the Babylonian exile, sent Israel away to a foreign land where the courage and character of men like Daniel, Shadrach, Meshach and Abednego was tested and proven. Miraculously, God spoke to Nehemiah and others to come and rebuild the walls and facilitate the return of God's people to their homeland.

The second scattering was by far more severe, as the temple was completely destroyed in A.D. 70, over five hundred thousand Jews were slaughtered and most of the rest were sent into the four corners of the earth.

Throughout history, then, persecutions and displacements were constant. Any Jewish community that did not assimilate would eventually find themselves unwelcome in the land in which they lived. It might take more than one generation, but invariably, as if God Himself were keeping them from settling in any one place, the Jewish community would fall into disfavor and be forced to flee.

Think about it—land, language, religious centers, families—all of it destroyed and scattered like ashes in the wind. Everything that we would understand as making up a culture was decimated in the Jewish people, and for nearly nineteen hundred years they functioned as a people without a land in the nations of the earth.

Why did they not assimilate? What kept them from being like any other people group on the earth? What made them different from the Assyrians, the Persians or the Amorites, proud peoples and races who have vanished with the winds of time? Alone and unparalleled in human history is the story of the Jewish people.

...AND GATHERED

The story of the gathering of the Jewish people back to their homeland is so sensational, so supernatural, that one wonders why we don't hear more about it. Amazing men, many of them completely secular, felt overwhelmingly compelled by an inner drive that Israel after centuries of dispersion must be restored.

Theodor Herzl, born in 1860, had no religious notions for launching the modern Zionist movement. He was a thoroughly non-religious Jew, completely assimilated into his culture. In fact, in his early years he believed Jews should wholeheartedly become one with whatever culture they found themselves a part of. Circumstances, however, began to work on him, and a prophecy whose time had come began to germinate in the heart and mind of this brilliant, but unbelieving, man.

In late 1897, in Basel, Switzerland, Herzl and other leaders convened the Zionist Congress. It was the first international convocation of Jews of its kind since the second exile of A.D. 70. Herzl would look back on that congress and remark: "If I were to sum up the Basel Congress in a few words, and I dare not make it public, I would say, 'In Basel I founded the Jewish State.' If I said this aloud, it would be greeted with worldwide derision. In five years, perhaps, and certainly in fifty, everyone will see it."

True to this prophetic statement, almost exactly fifty years later the international community through the United Nations gave initial allowance for the formation of a Jewish state.

The story of the rebirth of the language is astounding in and of itself. Dead for hundreds of years, another amazing man, Eliezer ben Yehuda, had a tenacious and relentless belief that the Jewish people of the Jewish state must have the Hebrew language to bring the eighty-some different people groups represented in the land together. Almost single-handedly he tackled what seemed like an impossible task—the rebirth of a language that had not been spoken in hundreds of years. Against all odds, and alone in history, this dead, ancient language has been reborn!

SIGNS OF THE TIMES

It is amazing to look at the parallel development of the state of Israel and the modern Pentecostal/charismatic movement. Let me walk you through the major events, starting at the turn of the century.

In the last years of the 1800s and first years of the 1900s, Theodor Herzl and other leaders spoke forth a dream that called for the restoration of a Jewish state in the historic homeland of Israel. These men gave voice to the hope of centuries—that one day Israel would go home.

At the turn of the century in Topeka, Kansas, and then in Los Angeles, California, the modern-day visitation of the Holy Spirit began that had not been seen in a wholesale way in the church since the Book of Acts. Today, the Pentecostal/charismatic movement is the fastest-growing religious movement in the world and has reshaped the face of Christianity in one century.

In 1948, the impossible happened. Against all odds, with tremendous international opposition and with a horde of neighboring Arab states ready to destroy them, David Ben Gurion signed Israel into statehood. Immediately she went into a war for her very life, and in events that can only be described as supernatural and miraculous, she came forth in victory.

In 1948 and the surrounding years, a fresh wind of the Holy Spirit blew through the now fifty-year-old modern Pentecostal/charismatic movement, and a tremendous healing anointing began to be poured out through many different ministries. America was deeply impacted as the power of the Holy Spirit manifested in tent revivals, major auditoriums and in the national media.

In 1967, in an amazing story of courage and military agility, the Israeli Defense Force pushed out the Jordanian Army and recaptured Jerusalem. Essentially, for the first time since A.D. 70, Jerusalem was again under Jewish sovereign control. Countless Jews streamed into the Old City from West Jerusalem, making straight for the Wailing Wall, where soldiers and rabbis alike lifted up their voices and wept in unashamed abandon now that their souls were comforted.

In the last years of the 1960s and early years of the '70s, a movement in the United States known as the "Jesus People" emerged, and once again a fresh river of God's presence was felt all throughout America. The Full Gospel Businessmen's Association and Woman's Aglow emerged, along with other organizations, and tremendous evangelism took place throughout the nation.

On October 3 and 4, 1997 (the Jewish Day begins at sundown), Israel celebrated Rosh Hashanah, moving into the year where they would celebrate their fiftieth year of statehood, their jubilee year!

On October 4, 1997, over one million men gathered on the Mall in Washington, D.C., as the spiritual priests of the nation of America and cried out to God in repentance, asking Him to forgive our sin and heal our land.

Coincidences? I don't think so. There is a divine drama being unfolded before our very eyes as the architect of history establishes His purpose in these momentous days of human history. Those "sons of Issachar" who want to have ears to hear would do well to be praying for the peace of Jerusalem and posturing their hearts toward what God is unfolding in the walls of this ancient city and in the hearts of this ancient people.

FIRST-WAVE MESSIANIC JUDAISM

The first church was Jewish. For decades thousands of believers saw themselves not as Christians, but as followers of "the Way" who were convinced that they had encountered Israel's true Messiah and that He was soon returning to set up His kingdom.

They did not stop being Jews when they came to faith in Messiah. They continued to live Jewish lives and observe Jewish customs. They celebrated the feasts and kept Sabbath. They welcomed the Gentiles who also believed in Yeshua and put very few limited restrictions on them, simply asking them to remain sexually pure and abstain from meat offered to idols. But they saw Yeshua as He was, a Jewish rabbi, a teacher, who they had come to believe was the Promised One, the Messiah.

However, the quickly expanding Gentile church and the supposed conversion of the Roman Empire under Constantine eventually caused great problems for the Jewish believers in Yeshua. Before long, this resulted in church edicts stating that if Jews wished to believe in Jesus and be a part of the church, then they could no longer culturally be Jewish. They were required to put away all the uniqueness of their Jewish heritage and fully assimilate into another culture, no longer distinct from the people around them.

Imagine! Jesus was fully Jewish. All the apostles were Jewish. The apostle Paul was a Jew through and through and maintained a tremendous burden for his people, even though he felt called to the Gentiles. But a few centuries later, Jewish believers were forced to renounce the very culture and context in which the message of salvation had been born.

THE SEEDS OF ANTI-SEMITISM

The seeds of anti-Semitism were planted in the church already when Jewish people were not allowed to believe in Yeshua and still remain culturally Jewish. Within a few more years, anti-Semitism was rampant in the church. Dr. Michael Brown has done an excellent job of documenting the church's history of anti-Semitism in his chilling book, *Our Hands Are Stained With Blood*. Suffice it to say here that throughout church history, though many remain blind and (it would seem) willfully ignorant of this fact, gross atrocities and hideous evil has been perpetrated on the Jewish people in the name of Christ.

Pogroms ravaged the Jewish people. *Pogrom* is a Russian word meaning "devastation." In pogroms throughout Europe and Russia, literal bloodbaths would take place as so-called Christians slaughtered countless thousands of Jews in town after town. These "Christians" locked entire Jewish communities inside synagogues and set them on fire. The Crusades produced absolute carnage as European soldiers invaded the Holy Land, killing Jews without thought or mercy. Theologians like John Chrysostom, Martin Luther and others fueled this vile evil with hateful sermons likening the Jews to animals, worthless except for cheap labor and servitude. Though these men were used powerfully to bring forth much good to the church, in this area there was incredible blindness and error.

Thus, in not honoring its Jewish roots, much of Christianity became a force for persecution and pain to the Jewish people. The seeds of this eventually surfaced in the mid 1900s in Lutheran Germany, where, it is recorded, German soldiers sang "Silent Night" during Christmastime while millions of Jews died in the ovens of the concentration camps. In not discerning the Scriptures, even passages abundantly clear like Romans 11, the church allowed the name of Christ to become a curse word to the Jewish people.

Is it any wonder then that we have seen so little salvation among the Jewish people? The Christian nations' history with them has been centuries of persecution, disenfranchisement and death. Why should they trust us?

SECOND-WAVE MESSIANIC JUDAISM

It is truly amazing then, with all the hostility of the past, to find that we are living today in the midst of the rebirth of the Messianic Jewish movement. In the past few decades it has come from being the smallest of seeds to being an established movement in America, Israel and the nations.

Our elder brother is risen from the dead! In eighteen hundred years of church history, there has been virtually no sizeable response to Yeshua—Jesus—from the Jewish people. And those who did respond were told they had to leave their Jewishness to be "Christians." Therefore, they simply assimilated into whatever denomination they were drawn to. But now all of that has changed.

SOME AMAZING STORIES

In the late sixties and early seventies in America, the Lord began to move sovereignly in the hearts of key people who became instrumental in birthing modern Messianic Judaism.

One of these dynamic individuals who helped to shape modern church history was Martin Chernoff. Martin Chernoff was a pioneer in the truest sense of the word. As a leader in the Hebrew Christian church, ministering in Cincinnati in the early seventies, Martin sensed the vision of the Lord for Jewish people to serve the Lord Yeshua as Jews. Little did he realize the results of this thinking. He faced opposition from all sides. To the Jews, he was no longer a Jew. To Christians, he was suspect as well. Facing incredible odds, he clung tenaciously to the Word of the Lord and the inner conviction of the Holy Spirit.

In her moving book, *Born a Jew, Die a Jew*, his widow, Yohanna, who stood courageously with him through these years of battle, recounts the incredible journey the fledgling Messianic movement went through. Today Martin's legacy is carried on through his family. David Chernoff is one of the primary leaders of Messianic Jewish movement worldwide and leader of Beth Yeshua congregation in Philadelphia, Pennsylvania. Joel Chernoff, a modern-day psalmist, has influenced hundreds of thousands with his music and continues to serve in strategic leadership positions within the Messianic movement.

Dr. Daniel Juster is another sovereign vessel the Lord has raised up to pioneer this End-Time move of the Lord. Dan, who is of Jewish descent, came to faith within the Dutch Reformed Church and essentially believed that meant the end of his Jewish identity. After graduating from Wheaton College and receiving his master's degree from McCormick Seminary, Dan was ordained for ministry in the Presbyterian church. It was during this time that he began serving in one of the Hebrew Christian churches.

Then, in about 1972, around the same time as God was dealing with the Chernoff family in Cincinnati in similar fashion, the Lord convinced Dan that it was right for Jewish people who received Messiah to be able to follow the Lord in the context of a Jewish life. For that decade, this was a revolutionary thought. Thus the Hebrew Christian church where he was serving transitioned to become one of the first Messianic Jewish synagogues.

In many ways Dr. Juster has served as the Thomas Jefferson of Messianic Judaism. A brilliant scholar, Dan has given clarity and continuity to emerging Messianic theological rationale through his extensive writings and teachings. Dan's clear thinking and breadth of spirit has served as a powerful bridge between the young Messianic movement and the church at large. Today, while serving as congregational leader at Beth Messiah in Gaithersburg, Maryland, Dan also oversees *Tikkun* (the Hebrew word for restoration). Tikkun is a network of Messianic congregations and ministries spanning the globe. This important network has also placed several emissaries in the land of Israel itself.

Through the lives of these men, their families and many others who have paid a great price, the Messianic movement has come to a place in just a few decades where a solid foundation has now been laid for future growth. In that short time, it has come from having just a handful of congregations in the early seventies to approximately three hundred congregations in America and around the world. It is believed that more Jewish people have come to genuine faith in Messiah in the last few decades than in all of church history combined. It was indeed a "sign and wonder" at the Promise Keepers meeting on the Mall in Washington, when the event opened with greetings from these Messianic leaders and the blowing of the shofar, calling the nation to repentance and solemn assembly. As Christians, we cannot underestimate the unparalleled importance of the rebirth of this movement. Not since the earliest church have we seen Jewish people worshiping Messiah in a distinctly Jewish context. As amazing as this is, it is even more incredible to see another sign and wonder.

IN THE LAND

Today, in the land of Israel itself, the site of the birth of the church, Messianic Judaism is growing. Painfully, with great opposition and difficulty, but nevertheless, steadily, this tiny people group is emerging.

Estimates place the number of Messianic believers in the land between five thouand and six thousand. Fifty years ago, leaders tell us it would have been hard to find more than fifty. Now, meeting in small congregations of thirty-five to fifty people, dozens of *kehila*, or congregations, dot the landscape.

Believers in the land face tremendous hardship. First, there is the difficulty just of living in Israel. This tiny nation, just fifty-one years old, lives under the constant threat of terrorism and war. The overwhelming diversity of the land causes much internal conflict.

But beyond that, there is the challenge of being a believer. A Jew who comes to faith in Yeshua can easily expect to be ostracized by family and society. "Anti-missionary" rabbis regularly preach fiercely against those who believe in Yeshua. Just recently, one congregation came under intense attack as a mob of orthodox Jews surrounded their building, keeping them inside for hours, throwing stones and cursing at them. These orthodox Jews accused them of kidnapping young Jewish children and baptizing them, forcing them to become Christians.

Politically, for the past several years an "anti-missionary" bill has been introduced to the Knesset (the legislature) that calls for even more curtailing of religious freedom. However, as God has promised, this has only served to work for the good of the Messianic community. Many Israelis did not even know there was such a thing as Messianic Judaism. Now through the publicity surrounding this bill and the international opposition that it has received, they have discovered that it is not just a few isolated Jews who believe in Yeshua, but several thousand in the land and tens of thousands around the world.

One of the saddest plights is to see how little of the emotional, spiritual and financial support of believers in the West really reaches these struggling believers. Every year tens of thousands of believers stream to Israel on tours. Many have a sincere desire to "bless Zion" and be a part of what God is doing in the land. However, very little of this support trickles down in any meaningful way to this group of believers in the land. One of Eagles' Wings prayers and goals is to raise awareness of this need and to be a conduit of blessing to this valiant group of believers.

JEWISH ROOTS

As I have grown in appreciation and understanding of the Jewish roots of my faith, a whole new world of understanding has opened to me. The only holidays that I used to understand or celebrate in terms of my Christian faith were Easter and Christmas. Even these holidays were clouded by commercialism and suspicion of pagan roots.

I have now discovered a whole new realm of holidays in seeing that the Lord has ordained feasts to be celebrated. Beginning to understand the symbolism and beauty of the feasts of Passover, Pentecost and Tabernacles has taught me so much more about the Lord's character and His plan. It also connects me in a powerful way to Jesus and His disciples. They celebrated these feasts! I begin to understand more the mind-set and culture of biblical times. I am under no obligation or law to keep these feasts, but I joyfully realize the added blessing that is mine as I tune myself to the biblical calendar.

I love being in Jerusalem on *Shabbat*. Friday afternoon comes, and the city is filled with last-minute bustle as it prepares for a twenty-four-hour rest. It is a custom to bring flowers to *shabbat* dinner, so everyone everywhere is carrying flowers. And suddenly, within the space of an hour, the city is quiet. Cars disappear and people appear, relaxed and calm, walking with their families, sitting on their balconies. Saturday morning, everywhere you look, people are walking to synagogue. A sense of *shalom* (peace) fills the air.

On Yom Kippur, the holiest day of the year, the silence is even more amazing. Absolute calm fills the land. People generally do not leave their homes. You hear no radios or TVs. The nation waits silently before God on this Day of Atonement. How powerful it would be if Christian churches tuned their hearts to these important days, not out of a sense of binding law, but out of a recognition that the God of Israel, whom we serve, ordained these days as an eternal memorial.

The ancient sound of the shofar has become a part of me. In its call I hear the armies of Joshua and David being rallied. I hear the prophets calling the people to solemn assembly and the watchman on the wall warning of coming danger.

ONE NEW MAN

> For he himself is our peace, who has made the two one and has destroyed the barrier, the dividing wall of hostility, by abolishing in his flesh the law with its commandments and regulations. His purpose was to create in himself one new man out of the two, thus making peace, and in this one body to reconcile both of them to God through the cross, by which he put to death their hostility. He came and preached peace to you who were far away and peace to those who were near. For through him we both have access to the Father by one Spirit.
>
> —EPHESIANS 2:14–18

Let me be clear. The early church failed when it forced the Jewish people to leave their Jewishness in order to embrace Christianity. I am not saying that we should make the opposite mistake, by forcing Gentile Christians to adopt some form of Judaism. Rather, it is vital that we recognize three things.

First, hideous and demonic persecution has ravaged the Jewish people in the name of Christ for centuries. Though we may never have participated in these things, and though we would never call these actions Christian in any way, nevertheless, they have left a seemingly indelible imprint of deepest mistrust on the hearts and minds of the Jewish people against Christians. It is time we as the Gentile body of Christ rise up in the spirit of Isaiah 40:1–2:

Comfort, comfort my people, says your God. Speak tenderly to Jerusalem, and proclaim to her that her hard service has been completed, that her sin has been paid for, that she has received from the LORD's hand double for all her sins.

Second, our elder brother, the Jewish expression of the church, has risen from the dead after centuries of silence. These believers are still young, still struggling, still developing leadership, but they are very much alive. Let us greet them with joy, not suspicion. Let us embrace them and have patience as we get reacquainted. Their expressions and forms of worship are different from ours, but our God and Messiah is the same.

Finally, there is great blessing gained when the Gentile church grows in appreciation and understanding of the Jewish roots of our faith. There is so much to be gained in terms of understanding history, community, worship and worldview.

In this hour, I believe the Holy Spirit is envisioning for us the bringing forth of the "one new man" of Ephesians 2:15. Jew and Gentile—distinct and yet complementary—in Messiah.

All of us are sons and daughters of our faith father Abraham, who looked into the night sky and saw the generations who would call on the name of the one God through his hearing, believing and responding to the word of the Lord.

What Now?

For group discussion:

1. Discuss as a group what you know about the Jewish community in your area. Are there any Messianic Jewish synagogues in your area?

2. Discuss what concepts about Jews or Judaism might be present in the group, perhaps from those who remember or had family involved in World War II.

3. Consider having a Messianic Jew share with your group some of the journey he or she traveled to come to faith in Messiah.

For personal application:

1. Pray for the peace of Jerusalem.

2. Find a Jewish calander and see when the next biblical holiday will be celebrated. Take some time to find out about the history of that particular feast.

3. Find a Messianic synagogue within driving distance and consider visiting one of their special services.

Epilogue

~

Something is happening.

There is a sound. A pulse. A deep rhythm is pounding forth. It is the cadence of heaven.

Something is happening.

The church is looking different, sounding different, acting different. There is an awakening of cosmic proportions in the nations of the world, as a "holy discontent" breathes divine restlessness into the hearts of a generation destined for holy adventure.

The church is beginning to embrace the kingdom. We see that we are really called to be sojourners and aliens in this foreign land. We are trumpets declaring authoritatively to the so-called kingdoms of this world that the kingdom of God was, is and will be. Though we do not see God's kingdom manifest in its fullness here and now, the earnest of its truth beats in our hearts and is growing as an unstoppable wave, gathering force and momentum.

You and I have been privileged to live in the most unique time in human history. Change is the norm for the world in which we live. Change—inward and outward—must become the norm for the people of God if we are to give an adequate, relevant witness of the changeless kingdom.

Change is not simple, but once you become accustomed to it, the process becomes easier. Our inward hearts, the deepest places, are being called to yield to the wind of the Spirit. This will result in arenas of conflict as what *was* clashes with what *must and will be*.

EMBRACING CHANGE

Whatever your position in the body of Christ, I ask you, as you complete this book, to prayerfully consider this call to change. The evidence is clear—from prophets to pastors, from statisticians to the evening news—God is calling the body of Christ—you and I—to radical change. Someone has said that the definition of insanity is doing the same thing over and over again and expecting a different result. It is time to rethink much of what we have been doing if we are hoping for a different result. This change will begin personally with the deepening of your personal revelation and walk with Him, as discussed in chapter 1, but it must affect every area of your life. You cannot say, "I am only one person. I just teach a Sunday school class," or "I just sing in the choir." Each of us as individuals at this pivotal moment in history is being summoned to fearless and wholehearted abandonment to Christ and His kingdom purposes.

The first step in this process is to admit the bankruptcy of what we currently have. That may be hard to do, especially if you are in a church or church position that is outwardly successful. But we are on a collision course with the Holy Spirit, who is the revealer of all truth and who is about to reveal the secret things that have polluted our hearts. A shaking of monumental proportions is at the door. Secular commentators with little religious interest at all realize the tiny thread that is holding together our society is unraveling and soon will snap.

There are several obstacles to be overcome in order to pursue change, especially at a leadership level. Essentially, they are all based in fear.

- *The fear of man*—dealing with many strong-willed and dominant people who use manipulation, control and intimidation to oppose change. This "soulish" pressure can place incredible strain on our lives.

- *The fear of loss*—loss of friends, loss of reputation, the fear of losing people from your church. If you are a pastor, you may have fear of losing your position as pastor.

- *The fear of failure*—what if I launch forth and it is all for naught? What can I really hope to accomplish?

- *The fear of deception*—questioning how one really knows if it is the Lord leading this way, or if I am simply caught up in hype and an overdeveloped sense of self-importance.

How will we overcome these inner, unspoken insecurities and rise up to be the army we must be in this hour?

THE FEAR OF THE LORD

He who walks daily in the fear of the Lord knows no fear of man. As the fear of the Lord returns to His house, we will begin to walk in the wisdom that comes from above. Political maneuvering and plans laid in selfish ambition will fall as the pure air of the kingdom's atmosphere fills our spiritual lungs. Once we have tasted of this quality of life available to us in the kingdom, we will never want to return to the isolation, bondage and spiritual boredom of the past. Though we may not see exactly the pathway to the Promised Land, we will know we are not going back to Egypt, and we will press on with fearless hearts, trusting the cloud of His presence to be our constant guide.

LAUNCH CODES

Have you ever seen a space shuttle launch? There is an enormous amount of energy applied as the rocket sits on the launch pad. Smoke, fire, combustion, fuel—an amazing burst of energy is necessary to thrust the rocket from its launch pad into the atmosphere where it can be released from the laws of gravity.

So it is with us personally and corporately. If we are truly to be transformed, we must apply the bulk of our energy to beginning that process. Here are some thoughts to encourage you.

Be ruthless.

Be ruthless with yourself. In your heart, you know what areas are genuine in your walk with the Lord and which are simply habit. Don't push the gentle voice of the Lord away, keeping Him at arm's length. Rather, invite Him to do surgery on those places where calluses have built up and sensitivity has been lost.

Be ruthless with your family and friends. Do what you must to break past the carefully constructed parameters that keep conversation and relationship from going to deeper, more meaningful levels. Be intentional about cultivating time where you and your circle of relationships can seek the Lord in prayer and worship in your home, not just in the church building.

Be ruthless with your church. Become a faithful person whose opinions will be heard and respected. Don't simply lament what is not. Be proactive and prepare the way in your congregation for what is coming.

Be passionate.

Don't allow yourself to live a life of distraction. Live your life. Don't let your life live you. Find ministries or relationships or giftings that you believe in and cultivate those in your life. Pull out of activities that might not be bad but simply are not world-changing activities. Plug into that which is vital and has the life of God in it.

Be relevant.

Know your city or town. Be aware of your neighbors and their lives. Follow the unfolding of the nightly news as an intercessor, praying into the situations you see, not simply despairing at them. Know that the faithful prayer of the righteous avails much. Discover a ministry on your local college campus and how you can serve there. Utilize the Internet to stay informed about prayer needs around the nations. Don't watch history. Live it.

Be compassionate.

Let the Lord break down walls of fear between you and unbelievers. Listen to their stories and be a friend. Let your life and your love be your sermon. Find ways to reach out to those elements of society that religious society would not accept. This is the clear example Jesus left us.

We serve a God like no other. He has privileged us to live in a time like no other. Let us join together and lift our voices into the desert of the human emptiness. Let us confidently and resolutely declare that He is, and He is good. Like Elijah of old, we are not alone. God has reserved "seven thousand" who have not bowed their knee to the spirit of this world, wherever it is found. There is a voice crying out in the wilderness, "Prepare the way of the Lord!" Let this voice be yours!

Notes

Chapter 1
Passion for Jesus

1. George Barna, *The Index of Leading Spiritual Indicators* (Dallas, TX: Word, 1996), 109.

2. Ibid., 35, 49.

3. Wade Clark Roof, *A Generation of Seekers* (New York: Harper Collins, 1993), 100, cited in Barna, *Index*, 86.

4. Mike Bickle, *Passion for Jesus* (Lake Mary, FL: Creation House, 1993), 57.

5. "Shout to the Lord" by Darlene Zschech. Copyright © 1993 Hill Songs Australia (Adm. in U.S. and Canada by Integrity's Hosanna!), ASCAP. All rights reserved. Used by permission.

6. "Holy and Anointed One" by John Barnett. Copyright © 1988 Mercy/Vineyard Publishing. All rights reserved. Used by permission.

7. "I Give You My Heart" by Reuben Morgan. Copyright © 1995 Hill Songs Australia (Adm. in U.S. and Canada by Integrity's Hosanna!), ASCAP. All rights reserved. Used by permission.

8. "Jesus, Lover of My Soul" by John Ezzy, Daniel Grul, Stephen McPherson. Copyright © 1992 Hill Songs Australia (Adm. in U.S. and Canada by Integrity's Hosanna!), ASCAP. All rights reserved. Used by permission.

9. John Naisbitt and Patricia Aburdene, *Megatrends 2000* (New York: Avon Books, 1990), 298, 302.

10. Barna, *Index*, 50.

Chapter 2
Ears to Hear

1. Jack Deere, *Surprised by the Voice of God* (Grand Rapids, MI: Zondervan, 1996), 19, 27.
2. Ibid., 167–168.
3. Mike Bickle, *Growing in the Prophetic* (Lake Mary, FL: Creation House, 1996), 101.
4. Deere, *Surprised by the Voice of God,* 130.

Chapter 3
Global Relevance and Release

1. *Kairos* is a Greek word for time, specifically a period of time characterized by good fortune, urgency and favorable opportunity. A *kairos* moment is typically one of short duration that must be seized or it will be lost.

Chapter 4
Living Stones

1. Neil Howe and Bill Strauss, *Thirteenth Gen,* excerpts from "Alone After School, A Self-Care Guide for Children and Their Parents" (New York, NY: Vintage Books, 1993), 65.
2. U.S. Public Health Service, cited in George Barna, *The Second Coming of the Church* (Dallas, TX: Word, 1998), 56.
3. U.S. Department of Education study, cited in Barna, *Second Coming,* 4.
4. William Bennett, *Index of Leading Cultural Indicators* (New York: Simon and Schuster, 1994), 83.
5. Barna, *Second Coming,* 8, 5, 7.
6. The Generation X poem was written by a pastor's son whom I met while traveling.
7. Floyd McClung, *The Father Heart of God* (Eugene, OR: Harvest House, 1985), 13–14.
8. James Rutz, *The Open Church* (Auburn, ME: The Seed Sowers, 1992), 47, cited in Larry Kreider, *House to House* (Ephrata, PA: House to House Publications, 1998), 21.

9. Kreider, *House to House*, 22, 19.

10. Ibid., 18.

11. Ralph Neighbor, *Where Do We Go From Here?* (Houston, TX: Touch Publications, 1990), 20–22.

12. Barna, *Second Coming*, 7–8.

13. Daniel Juster, *Relational Leadership* (Dallas, TX: Union of Messianic Jewish Congregations, 1996), 31–32.

14. Ibid., 33.

15. Kreider, *House to House*, 7.

Chapter 5
Creativity Unleashed

1. Naisbitt and Aburdene, *Megatrends 2000*, 52, 55, 54.

2. Editor Bargna Brunner, *Time Almanac 1999* (Boston: Time, Inc., 1997, 1998), 35.

3. Frank Fortunato, AD 2000 newsletter.

Chapter 6
One Body, Diverse Members

1. *Adam Clarke Commentary*, cited in *PC Study Bible* (Seattle, WA: Biblesoft), ver. 2.1.

2. Barna, *Second Coming*, 2.

3. John Dawson, *Healing America's Wounds* (Ventura, CA: Regal, 1994), 95–96, 98.

4. Joseph Garlington, *Right or Reconciled?* (Shippensburg, PA: Destiny Image, 1998), from the Introduction.

5. Dawson, *Healing,* 117–118.

6. Bennett, *Leading Cultural Indicators*, 103.

7. Ibid., 59.

8. Daniel Patrick Moynihan, "Defining Deviancy Down," *American Scholar* (Winter 1993), cited in Bennett, *Leading Cultural Indicators*, 53.

9. Dawson, *Healing*, 254.

10. Ibid., 254.

Chapter 7
Spiritual Authority

1. Francis Frangipane, *The Three Battlegrounds* (Cedar Rapids, IA: Arrow Publications, 1989).

Chapter 8
The Citywide Family of God

1. Rick Ridings, copyright © 1993.

Chapter 9
Abiding in the Secret Place

1. Richard Foster, *Freedom of Simplicity* (New York: Harper San Francisco, 1981), 3.

2. Herman Riffel, *Learning to Hear God's Voice* (New Jersey: Chosen Books, 1986), 48

3. David Trementozzi, *Holy Desperation* (Clarence, NY: Kairos Publishing, 1998), 11.

Chapter 10
A Heart for the Poor

1. Barna, *Second Coming*, 3.

2. George Mueller, *The Autobiography of George Mueller* (New Kensington, PA: Whitaker House, 1984), 8.

3. Mueller, *Autobiography*, 216.

Chapter 11
Restoring the Tabernacle of David

1. C.S. Lewis, *The Lion, the Witch, and the Wardrobe* (New York: Macmillan, 1950), 149, 64.

Chapter 12
Israel

1. Derek Prince, *The Last Word on the Middle East* (Lincoln, VA: Chosen Books, 1982), 35–37.

2. Lance Lambert, *The Uniqueness of Israel* (East Sussex, Great Britain, Kingsway Publications, 1980), 124–27.

About the Author

⁓

Robert Stearns is the founder and director of Eagles' Wings, a relational network of believers involved in a variety of outreaches and strategic projects around the world. A powerful communicator, Robert is in demand internationally as a conference speaker and musician. He graduated from Valley Forge Christian College in 1989 and served in a variety of ministry capacities before launching Eagles' Wings in 1993. He lived briefly in Jerusalem in the early '90s and has regularly related to many believers and ministries in the land since that time. He is the publisher of *Kairos* magazine, and he has produced five musical recordings. Over the past decade, he has ministered in twenty-five nations. Currently, he is based in the New York City area. He also spends a great deal of time in Israel.

You can experience more of *God's grace* & *love!*